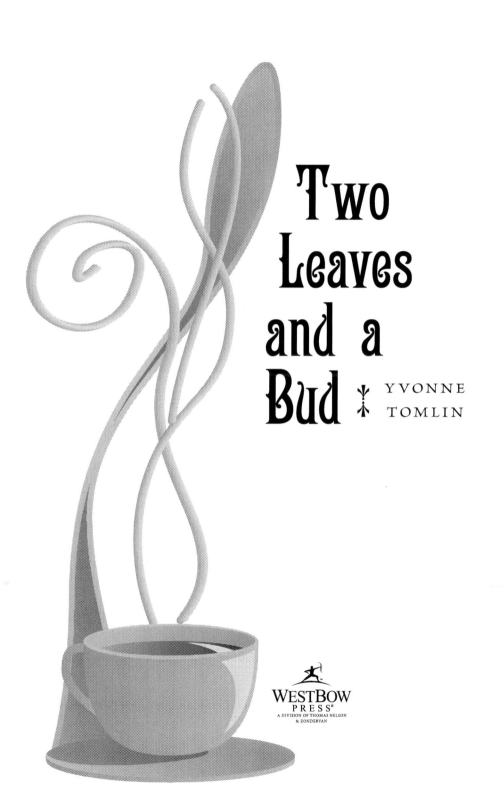

Two
Leaves
and a
Bud

YVONNE
TOMLIN

WESTBOW
PRESS®
A DIVISION OF THOMAS NELSON
& ZONDERVAN

WestBow Press books may be ordered through booksellers or by contacting:

WestBow Press
A Division of Thomas Nelson & Zondervan
1663 Liberty Drive
Bloomington, IN 47403
www.westbowpress.com
1 (866) 928-1240

All scriptures are from the KING JAMES VERSION (KJV):
KING JAMES VERSION, public domain

ISBN: 978-1-5127-7596-9 (sc)
ISBN: 978-1-5127-7597-6 (hc)
ISBN: 978-1-5127-7595-2 (e)

Library of Congress Control Number: 2017902169

Print information available on the last page.

WestBow Press rev. date: 2/16/2017

To my daughter, Casey and grandson, Thomas, and also to my mother, who never had an opportunity to know her own mother, who lost all contact with her almost immediately after she was born and left no trace for us to follow.

Acknowledgments

To my daughter, Casey, words could never convey my deep gratitude for your love and support in the undertaking of my story. Your dedication in helping me see this through, editing my words for hours, reading through line after line, reveals the true love you have for me and our family. The eagerness with which you have looked forward to learning about your small family's past is truly refreshing and my love goes with you as you read about our journey.

To all my friends, who have encouraged and supported me, I could not have gone on with my stories without you as my audience. Thank you for listening to my tales and to my quirky philosophy at times. Thank you for eating my Indian curries (liking them or not) and for pondering whether I was making all of this up.

Thank you to John and Rosa Rivera, my dearest friends. You adopted me as though I were your own and started me on the right track to accomplish my goals. I have immense love and gratitude for you always.

Lastly, to my family—my sister and brothers still in India and my brothers living in England—I thank you all from the bottom of my heart.

To my readers, I hope you find something in this book for you. If through the laughter and tears, you are entertained by my story, I have accomplished my goal. I hope you enjoy reading it as much as I enjoyed writing it all down.

Introduction

Careful consideration has been given to the title of my book. Two leaves and a bud are harvested to start the cycle of tea production. This is the lifeline of the industry itself. My grandmother gave birth to the first Anglo Indian in our family while working in the tea gardens of India. As I thought of her and the role she played, I was drawn to the two countries of my heritage. India and England gave birth to the Anglo Indian race. Although I was not privileged to have known either my grandmother or my Scottish grandfather, I know my mother struggled with her identity, as did I. I finally emerged from that emotional strain, able to accept the best from both worlds. I formed a bond of love and respect for the two, which I have passed on to my daughter. She has embraced her heritage with open arms, and I hope this book will answer the many questions she has had over the years.

It is said that only the small, delicate hands of the very young Indian girls were allowed to harvest the tea leaves when the buds first appeared. No other hands would be gentle enough to pick the "two leaves and a bud" necessary for the harvesting. I pictured my grandmother, moving slowly in the cool, misty morning on the slopes of the tea gardens, in the hills of northern India. Her tiny delicate hands would be fluttering through the four-foot high tea bushes, searching out the little buds, pinching them off, and depositing them in the small basket over her head. She would accomplish this without so much as bruising or crushing a single bud, or the remaining leaves on the bush. She would be smiling, with flashing, dark eyes and flushed cheeks, chatting to her companions who lived in the same village as she did.

This is my story of our family. My mother was abandoned as a child in the early 1900s, and she, in turn, gave up her own very young children in such similar circumstances. It is also a small segment of the much bigger story, about a legendary man, guided by his deep faith in God, who helped save Anglo Indian children in India when no other country was willing to recognize their desperate need of a future.

Chapter 1

My father was said to have been born in 1904, but no record of his birth was ever found. He was discovered at the age of thirteen in the streets of Calcutta, India, and lived in and out of an orphanage there. An older woman of foreign descent, possibly South African, claimed she was his guardian, but no documentation to that claim could be found. He had no given name and answered to no one. He spoke English but was also fluent in Hindi and Bengali, two of the main languages in India at the time. Not much is known about the first thirteen years of his life, and he himself was not forthcoming with any answers to questions put before him. If he did talk of his early childhood, the stories differed considerably depending on whom he was telling them to. We know that he never knew his parents, but his blond hair and blue-gray eyes, fringed with dark lashes, led everyone to believe he was of European descent. He was a handsome man, though not very tall, and managed to stay slim and wiry throughout most of his life.

Living on his own in the streets of Calcutta, he earned his living by running errands for the local shopkeepers and landlords, making himself indispensable to them. If he needed a place to rest his head at night, there was never a lack of folks opening their doors to him. He was street-smart, quick, and knowledgeable of his surroundings. The local residents of Calcutta relied upon him to fulfill any number of deals made in the course of the business day. This early pattern of relying on himself for his own needs seemed to form the foundation for his future life, and try as he might as a young adult, he was never able to put down roots or settle into any routine way of living.

My oldest brother, Ivan, put together some known facts of our father's teen years and young adulthood and compiled them into letters to me. Here are some revealing stories that were passed on to him by a Mrs. Rene Fernandis, a missionary housemother in Dr. Graham's Homes, Kalimpong, India.

According to her, our father was found when he was thirteen by a staff member of Dr. Graham's Homes. In time, he was transported hundreds of miles away to live in the remote hills of Kalimpong in a home for abandoned Anglo Indian children. When he arrived at Dr. Graham's Homes, he was christened and given the name James Oscar Hayes by the two daughters of Dr. Graham who were living there at the time. Everyone always called him Oscar, and that is the name by which I knew him all of my life.

Mrs. Fernandis mentioned that, although Oscar was a nonconformist and a rebel, he had very endearing qualities and was quite likable. He would often go out of his way to do a good turn for people. He had learned to exist in the slums of Calcutta and was wise beyond his years, trusting no one. The rigid rules of Dr. Graham's Homes, according to him, were for everyone else to overcome as they saw fit. Life was structured and strict. The children had to apply themselves to doing housework and going to school, but Oscar didn't intend to abide by anyone else's rules. Since he had not taken orders from anyone previously, he found life there was not suitable to him. Soon he was said to be difficult and unable to be taught.

His charming, likable ways and complete confidence in his own abilities not only saved him at times, but would also often lead him into trouble. In addition, Oscar possessed a fiery temper and had a very real problem with adult authority over him. The staff of Dr. Graham's Homes became wary of apprehending him, and the cottage staff gave up on their mission to convert this self-determined, one-man army. He was popular among his peers for standing up for what he believed in and came to the rescue of many children who were seeking to escape the confines of a strict punishment. Caning by the headmaster was still practiced here, but this was not a deterrent for Oscar, who at one time took the cane in his own hands and threatened to use it on the person punishing him. Everyone gave up on getting him to abide by the rules, but because he was still too young, they had no choice but to find a way to keep him at Dr. Graham's Homes. Eventually, he became such a problem that the principal decided it was necessary to isolate him from the rest of the children. He was taken out of the cottage and school environments and sent to work on the farm situated on another hill about two to three miles away.

The farm was run by a British manager and its residents consisted of dairy cows, goats, chickens, horses, and pigs. It was also home to two huge Australian bulls living side by side in separate concrete stalls securely fastened to the concrete walls by huge chains through their noses. Most of the farmworkers were local Nepalese people who made a living by taking care of the livestock and making daily deliveries of fresh fruit and vegetables to the cottages. Because Nepal was in such close proximity, most of the local people living in the surrounding villages of Dr. Graham's Homes could find work more easily outside their own country. The Nepalese people used a different dialect, which was not a written language at the time but has since become one. I found it to be different from Hindi, having a slight lilting cadence to it. And the people themselves seemed to be happy and pleasant most of the time.

The young women were pretty with high cheekbones, pink from the cold air of their mountain home, and almond-shaped eyes that looked out at you with curiosity and candor. Oscar was well aware of their charms as they giggled at his attempts to wrestle with a horse or avoid falling on his face in front of a family of pigs. At the age of sixteen, he was confronted with mighty temptations in the form of the sweet-natured Nepalese girls, who were just his cup of tea. It wasn't long before trouble brewed, as Oscar became more and more acquainted with one or more of the girls and soon found himself in front of the headmaster again. The staff of Dr. Graham's Homes had to throw in the towel, and the young farmhand was eventually escorted back to Calcutta, where he would stay until he was old enough to be inducted into the Indian Army.

At this time, the British were still very much alive and well in India, and the entire military was overseen by British officers. Soon, Oscar became Private Hayes in their army. During his sojourn, he was sent out to many military posts, traveling through the length and breadth of the country. Bombay, Poona, Chittagong, Shimla, and Darjeeling were just a few of the places he was stationed in. He met people of all races and from all walks of life, and he managed to seal some lucrative and lasting friendships. His reputation grew, and depending on the situation, it could be deemed good or bad. He was always known to accomplish tasks that most others could not, and the means of getting it done could be quite unconventional. Some of the northern towns like Shimla and Darjeeling were so beautiful in climate and surroundings that the officers made them their private rest and recuperation destinations. They established a very comfortable English country lifestyle and home away from home. Oscar, with his vast knowledge of the terrain, and fluent in most of the dialects, became indispensable to the officers in procuring what was needed and making deals, in which he made sure he was rewarded as well. His superiors would travel in style, experiencing scenic forests pungent with the aroma of mountain pine and other conifers, while taking in the spectacular views of the Himalaya Mountains and vast valleys in between.

However, Oscar's main headquarters was located in Calcutta, and while he was stationed there around 1930, it's very likely that he met our mother, Mary Esther Gollan. She would have been in her teens, having just arrived in the big city fresh out of a sheltered home—bewildered and in awe of her vast surroundings. He, on the other hand, would have been in his early twenties—a seasoned and confident young man.

After they met, Mary accompanied him to many of the beautiful places he visited. No permanent home was established, evidenced by each of their children being born in a different town. Each birth was recorded by a christening or baptism by the clerical minister of the British Armed Forces. My birth was not recorded in India, but I do have a baptismal certificate, where my birthday was entered and on which my father was said to be James Oscar Hayes, soldier. My parents together had seven children, of which I was the fifth. Their firstborn, a girl they named Jenny, died of cholera in the northern hill station of Siliguri very early in her first year. With her death, I became the only girl in a family of boys. I felt lucky throughout my life, and even now, to experience the tenderness and kindness that my brothers always showed me.

While Oscar was in the army, most of his duties consisted of servicing and repairing tanks and other armored vehicles. My brother Ivan remembered that, on one particular occasion when he was six, our father drove up the pathway and parked a huge tank in front of the house where they were staying. At other times, troop-carrying trucks, army motorcycles, and American-made Jeeps all made their appearances. Our father seemed to take on the army with a good deal of enthusiasm and loved the nomadic way of life, moving from one army post to the next. He learned how to disassemble and repair all types of vehicles, specializing in British and American models. He had a love affair with the American Cadillac and Buicks. I recall, in one of my earliest memories of him, I was seated on his lap as we cruised along in a long burgundy Buick, watching as everyone came out onto the street to see us go by. The local folk gave him the name Hayes Sahib (Mr. Hayes) and instantly recognized him when they saw the shiny car rolling by. He developed superb driving skills that were necessary in the rugged and mountainous regions of northern India, but his mechanical skills were also recognized as invaluable to all vehicle owners in the area. Becoming a masterful mechanic would benefit him immensely in the years to come, when he would be in full pursuit of providing for his family.

During the final months of his enlistment, he became a liaison for his superiors, which entailed his driving high-ranking generals from pillar to post. By this time, he was fluent in nearly all the spoken languages of that part of India, mainly Urdu, Bengali, Hindi, and Punjabi, and managed to acquire a perfectly polished Nepalese dialect. He found army life to be quite agreeable, and after ten years as a soldier, he left the army ranked as a staff sergeant. He had learned many skills and taking this knowledge, he was soon on to his next adventure.

Siliguri, a hill station in Northern India, was fast becoming a thriving little town. In the early 1930s, it boasted a fine railway hub, as well as a pasture on the outskirts of the town where a small plane could land. The British presence in India was quite established, and so was the up-and-coming Anglo Indian population, who worked primarily on the rail system and tea gardens, which were spread all over the rising hills. Here, Oscar was able to find some semblance of a permanent life—at least for a while—and this thriving little town became home to him and his growing family. He soon established himself as an entrepreneur and innovator of all things known and liked by his British cohorts. In order to provide for those dependent on him, he sold cigarettes, lighters, fancy cases, bracelets, watches, and all manner of items coveted by the Siliguri swells. Almost all British men and women were heavy smokers. The women soon realized they could be more free here than at home in England. They enjoyed puffing away on their long, jeweled cigarette holders, not having to think about English society frowning on them. Oscar did well for several months, and rupees were flowing in. But true to his nature, it wasn't long before he wasn't satisfied doing the mundane and sought bigger and better things to occupy his time.

He soon noticed on his many trips to friends' houses, he would see weaponry of all kinds either displayed prominently, or talked about with much enthusiasm. Guns, twenty two rifles, twelve and sixteen inch bore shotguns—crossbows, and the well-known kukri (a curved knife used by the elite Nepalese Gurkhas) were of primary interest, especially to the British folk. This observation opened up several ideas to Oscar. He organized "shoots" for the affluent residents, thereby filling a need—to help wile away the hours of the day and night. Both men and women would participate, but the British women especially took to the outings with great pleasure and enthusiasm. It wasn't the big game on their minds, which in itself was quite plentiful, but rather the smaller quarry, like pheasants, partridges, peacocks, and the ever-popular *kukra* (wildfowl). Quite often, a party of forty or more would participate.

These shoots would take place from October through early March, at a time when all the fields of rice had been harvested, and most of the game birds liked to scratch and scrimmage through the short stubbles of the harvested paddy fields. Early dawn was generally the best time, and Oscar organized these ventures into the wild jungle, giving meticulous care to safety. All of the hunters were told to keep away from the boundaries of the surrounding Terai, as too often there were leopards and tigers targeting the outskirts of Siliguri. This venture became very lucrative for Oscar. The sahibs and memsahibs (men and women) of Siliguri handed over their money and friendship to the increasingly popular Hayes Sahib. Not only did our father make money, more importantly, he managed to endear himself to the local guides and shopkeepers who supplied his excursions, earning their respect and admiration.

Oscar loved the Nepalese people. He treated them with respect and appreciated their intelligence, quick wit, and loyalty. He worked hard side by side with them and saw to it that not only did he profit from his enterprises, but they did as well. He in return earned their love and friendship, which lasted throughout his remaining years in India and was evident to me and my family even after he left.

Siliguri boasted a dispensary that was kept tremendously busy on a day-to-day basis, but there were no hospitals to take care of the seriously ill patients. Diseases like malaria, tuberculosis, and cholera to name a few, were rampant, and medicine was dispensed to mostly British patients. There were no vaccinations or immunization programs available at the time and dysentery seemed to attack the British constitution frequently. This was looked at as more of an inconvenience than an illness, and they were not going to stop eating all that delicious, highly spiced food they had just discovered.

The affluent Europeans in Siliguri lived an opulent lifestyle, some households having up to fifteen servants at their beck and call, and Oscar used everything to his advantage. On weekends and holidays, the British residents loaded up their Jeeps and Land Rovers and headed north to the cool mountains of Kurseong, Darjeeling, and even Kalimpong, about one hundred miles away. The Darjeeling Himalayan Railway, affectionately known as "Toy Train" and built by the British and Germans, produced a tough little steam engine able to haul about four scenic railroad cars. Its sole purpose was to take tourists up and down the mountain, traveling from Siliguri to its final destination at Ghoom, which was 6,500 feet above sea level. The spectacular scenery along the way would rival any place in the world, and the leisurely meandering of the train, moving at a snail's pace as it wound round and round the steep hills, was (and still is) a memorable experience known for its uniqueness and heart-stopping wonder.

I always looked at Kalimpong and the surrounding hills as God's gift to humankind, for he truly made it a Garden of Eden for us. It didn't take the British long to discover these pristine areas, and the extremely mild weather all year round made their escape from the steamy plains completely satisfying. Darjeeling, which was the most popular hill station at the time, provided the best in lifestyles, and the area fast became a haven for foreign military officers and rich tea planters.

My father was quite well known in all these areas, and his reputation for fun and hair-raising escapades brought him ever more loyal friends and new acquaintances. He was probably not a perfect member of the establishment, but he was known for the good things he accomplished for the Nepalese folk. They remembered him for treating them fairly, and their loyalty to him was unquestionable. You might say that Hayes Sahib was the one person they sought to settle their disputes, and when the subject of payment for services rendered involving the foreigners came up, Oscar negotiated for them, securing the highest price. With all this came his sense of humor, and although he possessed a fiery temper, the Nepalese folk were not often the ones it was aimed at. He never drank alcohol, and my mother always spoke of him as being kind, generous, and charming to a fault, and as long as they were together, she lived her life with him, joyfully and happily.

In 1930, Oscar settled into the town of Siliguri and made a home for his growing family. The two oldest boys, Ivan and Rick, were born in 1936 and 1938 respectively. The boys were recognized everywhere, and my older brother told me stories of how he could walk into any shop with his father and be offered tea and refreshments at no charge. He was well liked by the foreign folk as well, and was also making friends with the Anglo Indian train conductors and technicians. He traveled back and forth to Calcutta free of charge, having the blessing of a Mr. McGuire, who generously offered him a first-class ticket, knowing that Oscar would return with some cigars or other coveted item not found in their town bazaar.

It was in the mid-1930s that our father met a rather docile Nepalese man named Mr. Mahbuk, with whom he would establish a lasting friendship. Mr. Mahbuk's wife, when she met Oscar, took an instant liking to him, falling for his charm, and she was to become his staunch ally and friend. She didn't speak much English, being Nepalese, but she did understand a few words here and there. Mrs. Mahbuk was taken aback at the way he spoke perfectly polished Nepalese and picked up the name the local folk had bestowed on him. She loved to tell her friends how Hayes Sahib could make her laugh and kept her entertained like no one else. A rather large woman, Mrs. Mahbuk dominated her household, and half the town, and my father and mother both had an immense fondness for this Nepalese couple. My mother was accepted into their well-established household, where she was taken under Mrs. Mahbuk's wings, and her friendship with her benefactors blossomed. The couple owned vast acres of land and were property owners as well. Their annual rice harvest could have fed the whole town of Siliguri, and my mother found herself learning how to prepare rice and other Indian and Nepali dishes to perfection. Mrs. Mahbuk was a wonderful cook, and she preferred to prepare all the highly spiced curries herself, even though she had a house full of helpers. Whether the dish was wild boar meat, fish, or jungle fowl, there was no one to equal her. Spices, both Indian and Nepalese, were treated with reverence, and our mother soon mastered the art of blending everything into the classic curries and rice dishes that we all loved.

One of my most poignant memories of my mother is the way she always smelled of cardamom, cinnamon, clove, and bay as I learned the Nepali translation of the spices along with the English words. Considering that everything was cooked fresh and the spices were ground by hand, a classic curry could take up to four hours or more to prepare. My brother Ivan still remembers the inside of a fresh young coconut going in to the curry as the final ingredient just before serving, and the aroma that was released immediately afterward would have everyone running to the dinner table for a taste. Wild game was supplied fresh daily, as the paddy fields yielded wild boar and jungle fowl on nightly shoots. The homeless (mostly Anglo Indians] who were taken in by the Mahbuks were more than willing to supply their benefactors with the wild game, going so far as to build bamboo platforms high above the ground on the outer edges of the jungle. Wild boar especially made for delicious meals, and every night of shooting brought in results.

During the early 1940s while Oscar was staying with the Mahbuks, he accepted a job with a large fuel-hauling company, driving two thousand gallons of petrol all the way to Darjeeling about sixty miles away. At best, this was a hazardous undertaking, as it required crossing incomplete roads at times. During the monsoon months, the trip became treacherous, for at every curve and steep incline, the unexpected landslide could occur. The lack of barriers along the steep edge caused many drivers encountering the sharp curves to lose control. They, along with their vehicles, would slide down the embankment, plummeting eight hundred feet or more to the rocks below. Accidents frequently occurred, and some of the tea planters and their families lost their lives. Oscar drove his fully loaded petrol tanker, and though he knew the perils and negotiated them successfully, the trips took their toll, not only on the vehicle but on him as well. At best, the trip would take four to five hours, but with the constant overheating of the engine and stopping to refill the radiator, the hours turned into all day. The massive tea plantations were heavily dependent on this fuel to run their vehicles and factories, and even though there were risks, the arduous job appealed to Oscar's sense of adventure. His knowledge and experience in all phases of this job earned him a very good salary, and he was content to be close to his family and friends.

It seemed, though, that he became restless again, and the voices of the siren, namely Calcutta, began to beckon him back to her side. He left his family, which now consisted of my three older brothers; myself; and, of course, our mother, and boarded the train for the long journey to the plains.

In the familiar surroundings of this huge city, he set about renewing old friendships and making new ones. The social and nightlife was in full swing in the early to mid-1940s, and very soon, everyone knew that Calcutta's favorite son was back in town. At night, the talented musicians could be heard huskily crooning a popular song, and a four-piece band enticed passersby with their sultry, rhythmic beats. Park Street, where everything happened, was the center of life in those days, allowing for nightlife comparable to any other big city in the world. Calcutta at night could be magic. Gone would be the dusty and grimy sights of the day, the shadows hiding unwelcome debris. Cattle blocking the flow of traffic during the day now rested comfortably in nearby stalls. A rickshaw could be flagged down, for pennies. Visitors to this famous city could be taken on a whirlwind night jaunt to the fairy-like Strand. There they could see the huge ocean liners of P&O ship lines waiting for their passengers to arrive for the long trip back home across the ocean. The scene was breathtaking, with the ocean liners cued up and illuminating the night with brilliance from stem to stern.

The vibrant, humming city was a magnet to all, and it was no surprise to anyone that Oscar eased back into the cultural and social life as if he had never left. British and Indian alike coexisted to some extent in Calcutta, and of course our father sought out the best of both worlds. During this time, one of his greatest passions—exotic bird collecting—caught his interest and seemed to take over his life completely. He learned how to creep about the riverbanks of the Hooghly, where some of the birds would roost at night, burying themselves in the soft pockets of dirt along the edge of the cliffs. He studied their habits and was soon able to reach in the dark, lifting the birds right off their perches, without disturbing a sitting female, even though at times, he would get excited at having been able to secure a clutch of eggs. He gained a wealth of knowledge pertaining to the avian species, learning not only how to raise the young, but also how to breed the more exotic ones. People came from near and far to get his advice and gain from his expertise. The rare bird project became a profitable business for him and proved to be of great value when he took up life in England, where he quickly became well known for his bird collection.

My mother, who learned to love birds just as much as my father, used to say that he literally charmed the birds into giving up everything and placing their trust into his capable hands. It is regrettable that I was not able to sit down with Oscar later in his life to compile notes and recordings of some of the beautiful species of birds that had become his only passion. He may not have been able to relate to many people with sincerity and affection, but no one could argue that his love of birds was true and binding.

During his stay in Calcutta, the combined British and American firm of Walfords offered him a position in its sales department. Walfords was the sole suppliers of trucks and recreational vehicles in India, showcasing Ford, DeSoto, Dodge, and Chevrolet models. Oscar jumped at this opportunity, which again allowed him the freedom he craved. He would travel to deliver purchased vehicles, sometimes as far away as Darjeeling.

After a short period of time, he was anxious to leave, being less than enthusiastic about working for someone other than himself. The entrepreneur in him, beckoned once again, so he made the decision to go on alone.

Oscar's love of the hills and maybe his family as well brought him home again to Siliguri. With four growing children and Mary, he settled in with his family, renting a house for them, while he looked for the next money-making adventure. He met an Anglo Indian named Jack Switzer, and together, they saw the need for a means of salvaging abandoned vehicles along the treacherous road leading to and from the higher elevations. Many of them had fallen into deep ravines or had just been abandoned along a steep incline, far from a skilled and knowledgeable mechanic to assist with repairs. The task of lifting the vehicles out of their would-be final resting spots was a dangerous one, which required skill and knowledge of terrain as well as weather on the part of Oscar and his partner Jack. Getting the forest with its thick undergrowth to yield up its confiscated iron treasures was quite a feat. But the two knew how profitable the end result would be. It was not unusual to find some unfortunate occupant inside the wreck, for accidents happened, and without any communication system in place, travelers would be left on their own to make it out alive if they could. A few stories floated around, of some surviving after climbing back up to the main road, and encountering a local farmer on his way home from the market. They were the lucky ones.

The partners would haul their valuable finds back to their garage in Siliguri. They would completely repair and paint the vehicles and then sell the finished product back to the original owners, most of them tea planters and British businessmen. Oscar was traveling again to places as far as Assam, in northeast India, delivering newly renovated Jeeps and a Land Rover or two that were so essential in the rural mountains. The business was very profitable and the rupees rolled in. Sometimes, he would be given a vehicle that had broken down, and although prices were negotiated in most cases, the owners were just glad to be rid of the old eyesore. Oscar and Jack would then reap the benefit of a clear profit.

By now, Oscar had added the art of making a deal to his ever-growing list of skills he possessed. He was fair most of the time, dealing proficiently, but the partners almost always came out ahead while leaving the customer quite satisfied with what had just transpired. Oscar purchased a 1938 maroon Buick, which became his pride and joy. In between salvage trips, he provided a long distance taxi service to Darjeeling and the Teesta Stop for people of means. This was another excellent source of income, and with his and Mary's fifth child on the way, he was able to provide very well for the growing family.

In 1947, the two hundred-year rule of Britain came to an end in India, and under the Quit India Pact, initiated by Mahatma Gandhi, the Europeans boarded the trains and headed for Calcutta, where the ocean liners were waiting to transport them back to their own countries. Anglo

Indians, for the most part, stayed in India, but later there would be a steady migration to the United Kingdom and Australia.

Oscar seemed to settle down with his family, and the luxurious maroon taxi was becoming more and more prominent in his life. He would leave Siliguri behind and find lodging in the hills of Kurseong, thirty miles away. The impetus behind the move was the two oldest boys' need for schooling, which the town of Siliguri did not provide. Ivan and Rick were registered as day scholars in Goethals, a prestigious private school in the beautiful hills of this small, quiet, little town that was the first stop for the Toy Train from Siliguri.

Our new lodging was a bungalow, located in the middle of a tea plantation, and was quite comfortable and cozy. We were surrounded by tea bushes on the slopes around us, with little clumps of bamboo shoots sprouting up on the side of our compound. Ivan remembers those days clearly; he recalls gathering eggs in the morning that had been laid by our chickens during the night. If you stood at the edge of the compound and looked down into the valley below, you glimpsed the sparkling Bali Sands River, winding along to the hot plains in the distance. Somewhere along its path, this river intersected with the Rangeet River, a beautiful and peaceful place where we spent our days, picnicking and splashing in the cool water, under the ever-watchful eye of the nursemaid commonly known as an ayah.

Our family was happy here, at least for a short while, and I like to think that perhaps those days were some of the happiest in our mother's life. My brother Ashton was born here, so four children became five. Our father seemed to be gone for days at a time, but his homecomings were always joyful and full of surprises, and the rides in the Buick were the highlight of our lives.

This idyllic life came to an end all too soon, and in one of his letters to me, my brother seemed to think that it was along this time, the time of the Buick, that our father met up with another woman, a nurse who worked mostly in Calcutta. He would later become completely involved with her and her family and would abandon Mary and his five children, with another one on the way. Julian, the youngest, was born when our father had already left us. He eventually married his nurse, after having two more children with her, and they all immigrated to England in the early 1950s.

Without suitable funds, we gave up our cozy bungalow and moved into the ground floor of a two-story home owned by the Wilton family in Kurseong. An Anglo Indian of some means, Mr. Wilton had a rather large family, consisting of a wife, four girls, and two boys. They lived on the top floor above us. Friends of Oscar's, this family provided a roof over our heads when we had none, and over the years, after our family had left the area, I would run across one or two of the Wiltons, and our friendships would renew.

Later, after putting together what little we knew of our parents' relationship, my siblings and I could only conclude that everything went downhill after Oscar met the nurse from Calcutta. His visits grew further and further apart, and the funds he had been providing my mother dwindled down to nothing. I was still only four years old, and at this time, I was the apple of my father's eye. I adored him, and not seeing him come laughing through the door to swing me up to the ceiling was cause for a certain amount of apprehension on my part. I was crying more now and at times was unable to stop to catch my breath, turning blue, until my mother would grab me and gently slap me on my back. Even at this young age, I learned to accept the fact that, if my father did appear, he would be gone again the next day. Even when I was sick with a high fever, he would not come and bring the doll he had promised me the last time he was home. On one occasion, when he stopped in, I remember him asking me if I would like to go away with him or stay with my mother. Several months prior, I would not have hesitated to join him, knowing that I would have a glorious time in his world. But on that day, there was no hesitation on my part. I would always choose my mother. She was always with me, while he was not.

Our father's visits became less and less frequent until they stopped altogether, along with any financial help. Our mother began to depend more and more on the help of the Wilton family. The oldest son, James, took on the job of being a mentor to my two older brothers, who were seven and eight at the time. He also tried to help our mother whenever he could. There was no more money for my brothers' school tuition, so they dropped out, and the five of us children, along with our pregnant mother, were left to our own devices. We at least had one another, and while we played all day, we were unaware of the anguish and fear our mother was going through. Feeling totally abandoned, she sought help from the only place she knew of. She contacted Dr. Graham's Homes and asked for help for her children. I was four years old.

It wasn't until I was nine that I saw my father once again. By this time, we were living in Dr. Graham's Homes and had fully adjusted to the routines of daily life without our parents. I had just recovered from a severe stomach ailment, which had put me at death's door, and after almost six to eight months, I was back in the classroom, having lost a whole year in my education. Both our mother and father had been unaware of my illness, my mother being somewhere in the plains and my father living in his own world somewhere else. Here he was, cigarette in hand, sleeves rolled back, and laughing at my amazement at seeing him appear. I still adored him but was hesitant to go into his waiting arms, and rightly so; we barely had time for a photograph together when I realized that he was gone again. My feelings were bottled up tightly, and I understood that his leaving was inevitable, so I never questioned his farewell to me. The year was 1951. I didn't realize until later that this was the last time I would see him until I arrived in England in 1965. On reflection much later, I came to my own conclusion, right or wrong, that he had just washed his hands of the whole business of India and all of us in it, and moved with his new family as far away as he could. He would deny this to me once, when the subject came up, and I never questioned him about it again.

When I came face-to-face with him again on my arrival in England, in 1965, the changes in both of us were vividly evident. I was a young adult of twenty-two and hadn't seen or heard from him in sixteen years. I had a half brother and sister I was meeting for the first time. I was also welcoming the sight of my older brothers, whom I hadn't seen for several years. My eyes were riveted on my father. I noticed little things about him I remembered from my childhood. He was not as tall as I imagined him, but the gray-blue eyes were the same, and the high cheekbones were more prominent than they used to be. He referred to me as his "darling girl" just like he used to, but it was to my oldest brother's waiting arms that I went first.

My new brother and sister, seventeen and fifteen at the time, were friendly, and I warmed up toward them slowly. My half brother especially was kind and sweet, and we formed a good relationship quickly. My stepmother was not at our reunion, and I was glad of that. I didn't know what to expect, but my upbringing had taught me to be polite and well mannered, and that would have guided my first step to approaching her. I know that I harbored anger and resentment toward her. I also realized that up to this moment, I was still unaware of all the circumstances that had led to our father abandoning us so many years ago and of the part, if any, she'd played in those events. My stepmother and I would eventually meet, and we would always be polite to one another. I think she would have liked more of a relationship, but I was unwilling and unable to cross that bridge. Everyone felt the necessity to keep all the secrets to themselves, and circumstances and distance added to the difficulty of any of us discussing them.

Things did not go well for me in England. I was unable and unwilling to warm up to my stepmother. I treated my father as a stranger while I lived for a short while with them. I couldn't wait to leave and be on my own. Furthermore, I missed my mother and younger siblings back in India. It had only been a couple of weeks when things came to a head. I found myself leaving my father's house and moving in with my brother and his girlfriend, into their one-room flat. I felt let down and lost in this strange country. I had a temporary job, where the manager insisted on speaking to me in badly accented Hindustani, he being British and having spent a few months in India himself. I struggled with his bias against me being Anglo Indian and began to realize that I may have made a mistake in leaving the country I had grown to love. The weather in England was horrible, and I longed for the blue skies and sunshine of my home.

I would eventually leave England not quite six months after having arrived there and immigrate to America with my husband. My father never attended my wedding; nor did I invite him. My future husband paid him a visit the day before the wedding to ask him to attend, but the meeting did not go well, and he was impolitely shown the door. The only father I had truly known was my brother, and he walked me to the registrar. I could see that my father knew he was losing me again. He was experiencing the pain of losing a loved one, possibly forever.

My father, his wife, and his two youngest children would also immigrate to America, where they settled in California. In the late 1970s, he became ill with leukemia and was admitted to the hospital in Oxnard. His wife was on the medical staff there, and my brother Giles, wrote asking me to fly out from Florida, where I was living with my mother at the time. I took a week's absence from work and went to see our father, as his situation was terminal. When I looked into the now fading blue-gray eyes, I felt he was trying to convey something to me. Perhaps I was just hoping for something I could take back to my mother—a word of regret or the mention of her name. But it seemed the two of us were never alone for a single moment.

In spending those last few days with my father, I wondered what his thoughts were. Was he repenting and sorry for what had transpired so many years ago? Was he asking for all our forgiveness? As I sat with him, he seemed to find a certain amount of comfort from my being there. I couldn't stop myself from silently asking him how he could have given up beautiful Mary and their children to strangers or what drove him to abandon us. There must have been a reason; there had to have been. I was able to set the accusations and blame aside those last few days and remember him as he was when I was three and four years old. Though I desperately sought answers, I knew that I also might never get any. I thought about him as a child and how he was abandoned, never knowing the love of his parents, surviving on his own in a tough world, trusting and believing in no-one but himself. Did it all start there?

My father mentioned my mother in the final hours of his life—just a few short words about her goodness and having never done him or anyone else any harm. It was something I could take back to her, for I knew deep down she still had love for this man. I was on the flight home when he passed away. None of his and Mary's children was present at his death or funeral. When I gave my mother the news of his death, I glimpsed softness in her brown eyes, but she never spoke a word. It was difficult to sum up my feelings at his passing, and although I didn't feel a great loss for this man so rarely present in my life, I remembered the man I adored in my early childhood and felt heaviness in my heart for what might have been. He was eighty-two years old.

Chapter 2

In the foothills of the Himalayan mountain range, somewhere in the vast tea estates of India, on November 11, 1912, a little Anglo Indian baby girl was born. She would be the first of her race in her family. Her young mother, almost still a child herself, was barely in her teens. She, along with other young girls, would happily glide through the rows of tea bushes picking off the delicate leaves and buds to be processed later into drinkable blends of tea. Her tiny brown arms and hands would be exposed to the warm sun as they fluttered along, reaching out to the very tops of the bushes. The buds and leaves required skillful, delicate hands, so the menfolk did not take part in the task of harvesting tea leaves. This first, most important stage of tea processing was left to the would-be mothers and their companions. They would perform this task with quick and nimble fingers, laughing and chatting among themselves.

The little girl born here would have been given an Indian name chosen by her mother, but unfortunately the birth was not recorded, and the name of mother and child were lost. When "Daddy Graham" found the toddler and took her to Dr. Graham's Homes, she was baptized and given the name Mary Esther. The baby's father was Daniel B. Gollan from Glasgow, Scotland, who was sent to India by the British company Duncan McKenzie and Sons. He was sent out as a manager trainee to one of the many tea gardens owned by this company, most probably to the Duaars in the Darjeeling District of West Bengal, India. At first, he would have had a somewhat lonely existence. There were no neighbors. Nor were there any main roads to travel on. He would have felt like a prisoner marooned on his own plantation during the monsoon season, which lasted about three months out of the year. In his loneliness and isolation, he, like many of his fellow countrymen, would choose a companion from the young Indian girls who worked and played among the tea bushes. Our grandmother was chosen, but she was not the first for Daniel. Our mother mentioned a half sister, Alice, who had a different mother (probably from a different tea plantation, as the young men were frequently transferred around).

Daniel would have stayed about two years in India before getting a furlough back to his home in Scotland. We know only a very few facts. He was very young, barely out of his teens, and unmarried. His sparse existence when he first encountered the rural life of the Duaars would have been bewildering to say the least. His new home offered very basic lodging, consisting of a small, whitewashed house with one room and basic facilities in the back for personal hygiene. Electricity was nonexistent, and water had to be carried from the river up to the little house every day. Cooking and heating water were done with hired help from the nearby locals who lived in the village. Fires were lit by wood and kept going with solid cakes of dung mixed with coal dust. I have pictured Daniel going out alone every morning, not knowing how to communicate at first, and working through the stifling heat, humidity, and huge swarms of mosquitoes. He would work from dawn until noon, when he would take a three-hour lunch and nap and then return to work, not going home until well after the darkness of night had fallen.

Our grandmother would have played a prominent part in Daniel's world for a short while. The little half Indian girl, who was born with her beautiful, black curls; large, brown eyes; and olive skin, was to become a beloved child to him.. The stark desolate world of the tea planter would rapidly change later, giving way to lovely bungalows and cottages complete with gardens and ever-increasing better working conditions.

The little girl who was later named Mary and was to become our mother knew very little of her life in the Duaars. Unfortunately, in her very early years, her father Daniel had to return to his native home across the ocean. He would have parted from our grandmother and his cherished daughter, leaving sums of money and property to help them through. We know through our mother that Daniel did keep in touch with both Mary and Alice when they were in Dr. Graham's Homes. He would send frequent packages filled with gifts and money to purchase anything they needed. It would be several years before Mary's father would return to India, but my mother remembers seeing him on a visit he made to Dr. Graham's Homes when she was seven. By this time, though, our grandfather had found someone in Scotland, and a marriage and children soon followed.

Our mother said he kept up with sending the letters and gifts, and she came to the understanding that he and his Scottish family immigrated to Australia in the early 1920s. Not much is known after this, except that someone, from somewhere sent a telegram to Dr. Graham announcing Dan's death at a very early age. He would only have been in his late forties, and my mother remembers being fifteen years old at the time of his death. Before our grandfather died, he sent quite a substantial sum of money for Mary, which she thinks was put into a trust for her. She never asked Dr. Graham's Homes for the money but, rather, wanted it to stay there for her children.

Much later, when the grandchildren from India arrived one by one in England, an effort was made to contact Daniel's family in Scotland. I, myself, would have loved to see old pictures of our grandfather growing up there, and I wondered if my mother looked like him. Our efforts were met with silence, disinterest, and some animosity on Scotland's part, so we did not pursue the matter any further.

So what if anything was in store for our grandmother and what became of her? The trail left as to her whereabouts was nonexistent. After all, I'm sure she was at a loss as to what to do with a half British child in her native land, who was lighter of skin and looked different from the other babies. So it was that both our mother and father grew up with the absence of parents, and my brothers and I were never to know the love and caring of paternal or maternal grandparents.

By this time, it was well known in India and abroad, according to written articles and gossip, that young British men were an embarrassment to the good name of the Commonwealth. They were living with local Indian women and fathering children that had no identities and then abandoning them. For some reason, these innocent children took the brunt of the actions by British and other European members of society. British women especially were less accepting of the situation. There was no lack of gossiping committees and women's groups that thrived on bringing down their peers, and until British companies stopped sending out young unmarried men to be tea planters in India, this practice continued well into the 1930s.

The tea industry in India was thriving, but the changing times called for better living conditions and more advertising to make tea drinking more accessible and more appealing than it was. The British companies sought to make the northern areas of India very attractive to educated and established Englishmen and their wives. By the time the first married couples arrived to take up residence, they were offered newly built, airy bungalows, equipped with nearly everything they needed to live a comfortable and prosperous life. They solved the problem of having to send young apprentices out alone and, instead, started sending young men into tea estates where a British manager and his family were already established.

The Reverend Dr. John Anderson Graham was an outstanding missionary. He and a group of fellow Christians rescued and nurtured the forgotten children and gave them identities. Between 1914 or 15, on one of Reverend Graham's frequent trips to the surrounding tea plantations in the Darjeeling district, he came into a village where, through prior knowledge, he knew he would locate some abandoned Anglo Indian children. The exact name of the tea estate is still not known, but according to my mother, it could have been Punkabarrie, Ambutia, or any one of the vast number of functioning tea gardens around. Word would have spread quickly in the village, and the tiny, light-skinned babies and toddlers would be whisked away out of sight. Whether mothers were asked to do this specifically was not known for sure, but in all likeliness this would have been the case. After all, these were British missionaries pointing out British indiscretions. Sometime later, the Anglo Indians themselves thought the authorities both in the United Kingdom and within the tea companies had been too lenient on their fellow countrymen, and harsher consequences should have been meted out to the absent fathers. Dr. Graham's hands were somewhat tied because he depended not only on the charity of the tea planters, but also on the monetary donations of larger tea plantation owners and other big British companies.

The little girl peeking around the corner was inquisitive but shy. She was soon discovered, most likely in the company of an aging adult like a grandmother or older aunt. Her own mother was not on the scene and, as in many cases, had probably been transferred to another far away plantation, where she would be lost to her half Indian baby. The little girl's father, Daniel Gollan, had been furloughed from India and was back in his home country of Scotland. Dr. Graham, as he did over and over again, gathered all the abandoned children to him and transported them by Land Rover up to Kalimpong and into Deolo Hill, some sixty miles away.

At the first Sunday available, all the children were baptized into the Church of Scotland by Reverend Graham. And the little girl with the beautiful, dark curls; huge, soft, brown eyes; and straight, little nose was given the name Mary Esther Gollan and would one day become my mother. She was taken in her infancy and placed in the little cottage of Lucia King in Dr. Graham's Homes, where she was joined by several other babies and toddlers, to be raised by qualified missionary child care givers, mostly from the United Kingdom. This cottage was an important one, and the children, both boys and girls, would reside here until they reached the age of four. If you followed the path down the hill to the swimming baths, you would discover another little pathway behind the concrete walls of the pool that wound its way along sweet-smelling grasses and small fields of wildflowers. Upon reaching a little wooden gate, the tiny cottage of Lucia King would come into view, and you would be greeted with the sound of children's laughter and the soft cries of babies.

Mary would grow up strong and healthy here and, before she turned five, would have been transferred to McGregor cottage, one of the seven girls' cottages in the community of Dr. Graham's Homes. Here in the cottage, she would be under the influence of unmarried female missionaries, mostly from abroad, who were known as housemothers and were addressed as Aunty by the children. Mary lived with girls ranging in age from four to eighteen. Along with the other children, she learned to do her daily duties. This included learning how to make her bed and picking up paper and other debris on the playing grounds surrounding the cottage. She would be one of about thirty-two children living in the cottage. At the start of each new school year and as she grew older, her duties would increase, and she would have to become more responsible. By the time she was a teenager, she would be polishing and scrubbing to keep the cottage clean, waiting on the staff, learning to set an English table for tea, making and serving the tea, and cleaning the dishes and pantry as well. All this would be accomplished two to three times a day, along with prayers, and going to school.

Life for Mary during the week would be filled with learning scriptures, hymns, and prayers; performing her cleaning duties; and running down the pathway in her bare feet six to eight times a day to get to the school and attend her classes. After school and before her tea, she would participate in team sports or swimming meets. By the time she ate her soup and bread around five in the evening, after more work duties, she would have two hours of homework and reading still left to do. All the lights in the cottage would be turned out by 9:00 p.m.

Saturday mornings would be given over totally to scrubbing and cleaning silverware and polishing wooden floors. The cottage would be sparkling and open to the beautiful, clean air and sunshine, where it nestled on its little hill. It consisted of a kitchen, a scullery with larder, a large dining room, a dressing room, a toilet area, a stone washroom for bathing, and a staff sitting room and pantry, all on the ground floor. The upstairs, which was accessible by a highly polished wooden stairway and carved banister, would open onto a landing or hallway. This area had mahogany floors, which were polished by hand to a glass-like finish. The landing supported a staff bath and dressing room, a toilet for the girls, a teacher's room, a room for each housemother, and two dormitories with sixteen beds where the girls slept.

The cottages were almost identical in construction, and each one was surrounded by deep, wooden verandas on three sides, which made it very pleasant to sit outside on good weather days. During the spring, each cottage would be bursting with a colorful flower display as you approached it from the front. The flower show held every spring, gave way to fierce competitions among the cottages for the best of show. Prizes would be awarded as everyone participated in individual flower arrangements and best baked goods, such as pies and scones, best jams and best pickles. The cottage with the best overall garden for the year was awarded prestige and a large shield to display proudly. Later on, in my time there, visitors came from all over India just to see the flower gardens and judge the competition. It would have been a very happy and uplifting experience especially for the children, as it was for me years later.

Mary experienced life in a carefree manner and didn't seem to mind the somewhat harsh work and plain food. In my few conversations with her about her life in Dr. Graham's Homes, she said she was content and heard from her father often. She never mentioned her mother and seemed to have no memory of her whatsoever. She didn't show any interest in trying to locate her mother. When I asked if she wanted to, the shrugging of her shoulders made me very sad at the possibility that her own mother had never made any attempt to find her little girl.

Life in the early days at Dr. Graham's Homes was idyllic for the most part. They had fewer children then; Daddy Graham was still alive; and, for a short while, so was his wife. Mary experienced firsthand the love of a father for his children. She seemed to have had a very pleasant existence in those early days at Dr. Graham's Homes. When I came to know my mother in my late teens, I found her to be very knowledgeable and intelligent. In our conversations, she had only kind words for the home she knew as a child and for the beloved figure at the head of it all.

In Mary's time, Daddy Graham would use Sunday as his family day. After preaching a rousing sermon from the pulpit in the little stone chapel named for his wife Kathryn, he would have a staff brunch around noon and mingle with all the aunties from the cottages. After a short rest in the afternoon, he would ride his pony down from Jubilee House up on the hill and visit every one of his children's cottages. The children would be expecting him, and when he arrived at McGregor Cottage, Mary was among twenty or so children waiting to greet him. He would have interesting stories to tell and little surprises in his pockets. He made sure no one was left out if he or she didn't want to be. As a special treat, he would give the children rides around the compound on his pony, and squeals and laughter filled the air. This was a time for the children to let down their hair and take a small reprieve from the sometimes dreary daily life of duties and studies.

The short visit would fly by. Mary would wave as Dr. Graham mounted his pony and rode away to the next cottage. She would watch his head bobbing in and out of the trees until she could see him no more. Sundays were special days for her. After Daddy's visit, Mary would spend a couple of hours playing. Some of the children would write letters if they had a sponsor from the UNICEF organization, or the time would be spent trying out new hairstyles and just sitting with friends. Sunday tea was also special. There would be a cake with icing (most of the time), which was shared among all of the children. With all of the prayers and church on this day, the children would still have to participate in a sing-along with hymns chosen from the hymnals provided to each cottage. The beautiful voices of all the Anglo Indian children raised in harmony was so melodic and angelic in its quality that people came from miles away to attend the choirs and recitals. Daddy Graham used many recorded recitals of the most beloved of hymns to further his charity work abroad, and the joyful noise of the children singing in perfect harmony helped to melt many a frozen heart overseas. Without charities that developed in the wealthy Commonwealth, his work in Dr. Graham's Homes could not and would not continue.

The overseas committees stepped up their efforts, and the British dug deep into their pockets, so if the children could help in any way, this was one of them. Mary joined in and sang with her heart, learning to choose her favorites and requesting them shyly at the group sing-along. Life for her was idyllic, and she didn't seem to run into many obstacles or have any deep emotions about her parents. She didn't talk about her parents much, so we children were never to know her inner thoughts. Christmas holidays came and went, with Mary spending them all at Dr. Graham's Homes. She never had a home to go to for the holidays, so like most of the other children, she would spend a couple of winter months learning to knit and sew and catch up on her reading. She would experience the joy of a freshly cut fir tree being delivered a couple of weeks before Christmas, and she would also help decorate it, making paper chains and silver paper stars. The years flew by with Mary secure in her own little world. With her shyness and sweet personality, life posed no problems for her, and she was allowed to grow up healthy, strong, and well adjusted to her surroundings.

When Mary reached her seventeenth birthday, two years shy of graduating she was placed in the toddler's nursery, Lucia King, at Dr. Graham's Homes. She stopped attending classes at school, and for a little over a year, she was given training in child care. This was to prepare her, somewhat, for her exit from Dr. Graham's and give her a start in life on her own. After she turned eighteen, and with her new Bible that was given to her by Daddy Graham, she said good-bye to the only home she had ever known. She found herself in the big, dusty, hot, and overwhelming city of Calcutta. Up until now, she had only heard stories of this mysterious and dirty, albeit exciting place. She was given the means to find herself a post in an affluent household, preferably an English one, where she would teach and care for the children in the home. Young Anglo Indian graduates from child care training were in great demand among the British, and those from Dr. Graham's Homes were especially sought out because they were educated and spoke fluent English, as well as Hindi, the local language.

Mary wanted more independence and signed up for a class in stenography, in the meantime staying at the Salvation Army with very little expense to her. Before her nineteenth birthday, in this big, bustling, hot, dirty city, Mr. Oscar Hayes would discover her and, without any delay, proceed to charm his way into her heart.

Did Mary know anything of life away from the shelter of Deolo Hill? She was naive, scared, and unsure of herself, with no family of her own, surrounded by people who she would have looked at with trusting eyes. From following rigid rules and being told what to do and when to do it, she found herself on her own, making the small decisions she needed to survive. There was no one to turn to now. She struggled, but did not find typing and shorthand to her liking. She found herself taking to mathematics and thought maybe bookkeeping was a more apt path for her career search.

The decisions were taken out of her hands when she met a dashing soldier, sure of himself, confident, and seemingly established in this difficult world of hers. He knew everyone everywhere and, most of all, he was very charming. She felt herself floating on air, and I know with certainty that, for her, it was love at first sight. My mother talked of Oscar Hayes with fondness and a soft look in the depths of her brown eyes. He never spoke a harsh word to her in all of their fifteen to sixteen years together. He was generous and giving in all things. Those memories of their early years together were what she chose to remember most, rather than dwell on his later actions.

Oscar was twenty-six or seven, a seasoned and well-traveled person of some standing in the community of Calcutta and its surrounding areas. He was well into his adult life, which in his case, started at the very young age of thirteen, in this very great city. In 1925, Calcutta was an exciting place to be. The British were still very much alive in India and fully ensconced in the social and thriving, bustling city. There were pageants and displays of military splendor, and the Indian, as well as English, military forces were everywhere.

The very popular and well-known Bengal Lancers was formed, and this smart, precise group of soldiers on their beautiful steeds almost took your breath away when they passed by. They were then and still are the queen's own guard and form an integral part of the royal entourage. The troops in this brigade were made up of soldiers from the Anglo Indian race, as well as Indians, and were a source of pride and accomplishment during both World War I and World War II.

Oscar, by now, was a staff sergeant in the Indian Army, which was comprised of mostly British officers. With his vast knowledge of terrain and language, he became a liaison for the commanding officers. He had free range to drive any vehicle at his disposal, and with his affluent contacts, he was able to travel in the illustrious company of the elite. I'm not sure of the exact time and place of the meeting, but it was soon after their meeting that Mary packed her few belongings, positioned herself sideways behind Oscar on his huge BMW, and was literally whisked away by her knight in shining armor. When I asked my mother what life was like with my father, she said they lived from day to day, never thinking of what might happen next. They traveled extensively in India, as evidenced by the birth of their children, who were all born in different cities.

One of the very first places Oscar took Mary was to the thriving town of Siliguri. Nestled in the foothills of the Himalayas, this town was steadily becoming well known throughout India as a hub for all routes leading up to the surrounding mountains and small independent countries that bordered India. Places like Bhutan, Sikkim, Gangtok, Tibet, and Nepal were accessible from Siliguri, either by train or rugged Land Rovers and buses. The huge steam engines of the Indian Railway System traversed in and out of this busy town, stopping to pick up and unload passengers to and from Assam, Gauhati, and Shillong and transporting them back down to Calcutta and Bombay. The Toy Train had only a couple of tiny steam engines with a handful of cars attached to them. It would carry supplies and passengers straight up the mountain to places like Kurseong, Darjeeling, and Ghoom, which would be the last stop at 6,500 feet. Siliguri's population was made up of all ethnic peoples indigenous to India and was also home to a growing British community. It was still lacking in many of the needed amenities, such as and electricity and running water, but it wasn't long before these would also become available.

Mary soon became acquainted with all of Oscar's friends, especially the Nepalese couple Mr. and Mrs. Mahbuk. Since Oscar was gone so much, the Mahbuk home seemed to be where she stayed most of the time. Her half sister Alice (older by only a few years) had her own mother and still lived in the Duaars. She and Mary corresponded through letters now and then. Alice made it known to Mary that she was not happy with the lovers' union and threatened to cut off all affiliations with Mary if she did not leave Oscar. His reputation of trifling with women's hearts was legendary. Whether or not Alice was speaking from experience, to Mary, the decision was easy, and she made it quickly. She would stay with this man who promised to love and care for her. Sadly, Mary and Alice parted ways never to hear from each other again. My mother lost the only person she knew who was family and somewhat familiar to her. Oscar would become her mate and companion for several years to come, and all the while, she was less than a hundred miles away from her home on Deolo Hill in Kalimpong.

In the years to follow, Mary and Oscar would have seven children between them. They traveled extensively, going from coast to coast and to the north and south of India. Oscar was affiliated with the army until the British left India in the mid 1940s. Mary's first child was born in Siliguri, and here she was to experience the tragic death of her firstborn, Jenny. Disease was rampant in India, and Jenny was probably victim to one of them. Diseases like cholera, small pox, malaria, tuberculosis, and scarlet and yellow fever took the lives of numerous people, mostly children. For a new young mother trying to protect her young child, there would have been no defense against these illnesses. When Mary was in Dr. Graham's Homes, she would have been inoculated every year to guard against an attack of any disease and would have also had the clean air and water provided by a man-made reservoir at the very top of Deolo Hill.

My mother never spoke of Jenny's tragic death. It was Ivan who eventually disclosed it to me when I was well into my adulthood, after my mother had passed away. I can only imagine the sadness my mother experienced at this loss, and I especially hope with all my heart that, during the loss, my father was with her and not off on one of his escapades he found so necessary to take throughout his life. Knowing my mother, she would have stood the test and moved on, accepting it as God's will and letting go. Sometimes I wonder, though, did she just lock it away in her mind and heart as a closed book, never to be opened again by her or anyone else, like she did with all of the sadness in her life? However Mary handled the passing of Jenny, life continued on.

Oscar's world was ever changing. Soon there was more traveling, and more children appeared on the scene. From 1936 to 1946, six more children would be born in different parts of India. I, myself, was born in Dhond, an army post in the hills of Poona, just north of Bombay. The oldest was Ivan. Then came Rick; Mitchell; me, Yvonne Kathleen; Ashton; and, lastly, Julian.

I know we were all well looked after and were a close-knit family, even though our father would be gone so very often. Our mother was always there with us, but our father provided substantially for our well-being. Although the family traveled around while Father was still in the army, Siliguri seemed to be the home for our parents and us, and we returned there often. My mother thrived and enjoyed her life with Oscar. His status as an outstanding citizen of the community was legendary, and as far as I know, he was true to our mother during these years of their being together. Did he marry my mother? It's difficult to say. Neither Ivan nor I have been able to locate a marriage certificate or a divorce decree. Records in India, in those days, were almost nonexistent, but my baptismal certificate, signed by the chaplain to the British Forces, shows that both my parents had the same last name, Hayes. My mother never mentioned a marriage, but I assumed all my life they were legally wed. I also assumed there had been a divorce. If this was not the case, I am glad that I did not have to struggle with this knowledge throughout our difficult school years. Trying to talk to our mother when she was with me in America was one of the most difficult undertakings I have ever experienced. There was so much I wanted to know. What was it like being with him? Did he love her? Did she have a beautiful life with him? How was he able to leave her and us? There were so many questions and so few answers. I found it very difficult to ask her to live through all the sad details of her past. I did not possess the words I needed to garner the combined inner strength and gentleness it would require. I crumbled under the huge weight of the emotional strain, not only on her, but on myself as well.

I give so much love and gratitude to Ivan, who always made room for the little sister to join in all the boys' games. I learned how to fly a kite—not only how to get it in the air, but also how to build one first. Ivan taught me how to choose the best ones at the dokhan in the little bazaar in town. To paraphrase my brother, Indian kites were the best in the world. They flew higher due to the lightness of their construction and design, sometimes a mile into the sky, and a skillful flyer like my brother could bring down any other kite in a matter of minutes. We still fly kites together when I visit him in England, and it is still a joy to me to hear him coach me along as he used to so many years ago. I learned how to play marbles, capturing and winning points against the boys. One of my favorite sports was soccer. But best of all, I learned how to make a handheld slingshot. This allowed me the privilege of going out with all my brothers and exploring the nearby woods, where we used these treasured devices for target practice. We encountered an abundance of monkeys, rare butterflies, and even more rare species of birds.

The one activity in which I would not participate was that of chasing a rare butterfly with a net. If caught, the poor creature would soon end up with a pin sticking through it, displayed in a glass case on the wall. The girl I was became squeamish and looked the other way. My brothers had the most spectacular, award-winning collection of rare butterflies and stamps. Some of the butterfly collection was donated to a museum later in their lives, and they are all very much saddened by this pastime that was so prevalent in India. The practice of creating great collections of rare species was rather encouraged, especially by the Europeans, and the topic of harming rare species into extinction was never taught in any of the children's classes at school.

With all of the hobbies that kept him so busy, my oldest brother never left me out of anything. I was never left behind alone to play with my dolls, and throughout school, after we lost contact with our parents Ivan was the glue that held us all together. He became our beacon, and our hope that all would be well.

Although those last ten to twelve years seemed to be the happiest for all of us, our father spent less and less time with his family. His trips kept him away longer, where days became months of his being absent from our lives. It was sometime around 1948 that Oscar made another one of his trips to Calcutta and stayed away for an unusually longer time—much longer than he had any of his previous trips. I think of Calcutta in those days as being like a beautiful siren from ancient Greek mythology, beckoning him into her arms over and over again. He met our future stepmother there and became fully ensconced in her life and that of her family.

The beginning of a new chapter in my mother's life was about to begin, and she would experience a sense of loss and abandonment from the one person she trusted above all others. At last, my mother would regret not heeding her sister's warning, and she would now be on her own to sink or swim, all the while thinking of six little souls who were now totally dependent on her. Without suitable funds we gave up our cozy bungalow and moved into the ground floor of a two story home owned by the Wilton family in Kurseong. An Anglo Indian of some means, Mr. Wilton had a rather large family consisting of a wife, three girls, and two boys.

The Wilton family, was kind to us, but there was no money for rent and very little food to go around. I will always be grateful for the help they gave our mother during those difficult years in Kurseong. Mr.Wilton, who everyone called "Tich," was an established business man in the immediate area and also in Siliguri, thirty miles away. He kept mother informed of Oscar's whereabouts and activities, including his latest affair in Calcutta. The Wiltons would remain lifelong friends of our family, and many years later, after long absences we would all meet again from time to time and relive old adventures. The oldest son, James, became a mentor to Ivan and Rick, and they could be seen in the older boy's company every day. Sadly James was involved in a tragic accident in his later years and was run over by a heavy oil rig that backed over him. The Wiltons left India in the early 1960s and relocated to Australia.

I remember our father visiting us at the Wilton's home a few months after Ashton was born. He stayed only a few days and tried to take me back to Calcutta with him. My mother refused to let me go. Although it was exciting to see my father—he was always so full of life and laughter, I was given a choice at this very young age, of going with him and I chose to stay with my mother and brothers. I must have sensed I would have eventually become a liability in my father's life, and he would have dropped me back on my mother's doorstep after a short time. He left quickly, and soon after he was gone, my youngest brother, Julian, was born, the last child our parents had together.

Our mother held on to us for as long as she could while Oscar still sent her some money. He was absent again for the birth of Julian, and still to this day, I am positive he never laid eyes on his youngest child. Ivan and Rick stopped going to school, which I'm sure, at the time, was the greatest event of all.

With Julian just barely a year old and mother at her wit's end, she turned to the only place she knew of and sat down to write a letter to Mr. Purdee, one of the few remaining contacts she had at Dr. Graham's Homes. He was one of the original missionaries involved with building all the homes, and he remained there after the passing of Dr. Graham in 1944. Mr. Purdee was immediately at mother's doorstep. This kind man, who had been so close to Daddy Graham and carried on his work in Dr. Graham's Homes, was a lifesaver to many lost and abandoned children. All six of us were immediately accepted into his open arms and were given a home some sixty miles away from our mother and everything else we knew and loved.

We were soon safely out of harm's way and were being cared for at Dr. Graham's Homes. I can envision now how poignant and sad it would have been for our mother to realize that history was, in so many ways, repeating itself for her as she looked back at her own abandonment so many years ago and at finding herself on the doorsteps of Dr. Graham's Homes.

At the same time that we were taken to Dr. Graham's Homes, our mother was given a letter with contact information for a new employer. She went to meet an affluent Indian couple in Calcutta and took up a position as governess and teacher to their young five-year-old daughter. For our mother, this was the best medicine. Her new position allowed her to adjust to life without us; she used her thoughts to concentrate on the new task at hand. I am convinced that, at this moment in time, because of the deep unhappiness in her, she ceased to smile. The sadness in her lovely brown eyes would forever be there, and because it was indelibly marked on her soul, it was apparent when anyone met her for the first time. In later years, I would meet many of mother's and Oscar's old friends, and all would say that, when she parted from her children, the sweet smile was gone and she would always be referred to as Mona Lisa, because of the rare smile they would try to elicit from her. The occasions for laughter and joy were few and far between. I once witnessed her laughing hard at the antics of Ashton, who was very bright and a comedian at times. He could imitate many of the popular characters from the newest movies.

Our father was notified of what had transpired by letter from our mother. His answer to his children being taken into Dr. Graham's Homes was that God had a way of providing. My mother saw him briefly on her trip to Calcutta, and it is quite possible that she met our future stepmother there. Our parents kept in touch with each other occasionally, at least up until the time Oscar married his bride and his last two children were born. Mother left with her new employers for the city of Kanpur, and this trip took her farther than she had ever been without her friends and her children.

I didn't see my mother again until I turned sixteen, when she re-entered my life with a new sister for me. This also marked the point when I vowed never to part from her again. I was older now, and much had transpired in all the years she had been away. She was stayed with the family who'd employed her for many years, and she traveled extensively with them. They grew to love this lovely, quiet, and sad lady, and she in return gave them her loyalty and hard work. When her travels took her to Europe, the opportunities for her to stay and not come back to India were numerous, but her children were always on her mind, and it was always in her heart and soul to be with them again.

At one point, when she was in England, and Oscar was too, he wrote and asked her to stay there, where he could still have her in his life. Mary was cured. She refused to trust anyone in her life anymore. I asked Mum why she never married again, because I know of several friends I met later who would have jumped at the chance and who did ask. But with the usual shrug of her shoulders she avoided the question. Her children were always foremost on her mind. Without her saying it, the thought of her trusting someone explicitly again was out of the question, and she had no more of herself to give.

When her contract was over and her little charge in Kanpur was old enough, it was with great sadness her employers let her go. They were good to our mother and treated her well. They would have liked nothing better than for her to stay, offering her funds and a position, but there was no hesitancy on her part. She had teenage children far away, and she ached to see them. She made her way back to Siliguri again in the mid 1950s and was given lodging again with her friends Mr. and Mrs. Mahbuk. This time, Mother was more than a guest. She took up bookkeeping duties and helped out in numerous ways. No money exchanged hands, so Mum was still at a loss financially. All the while, her children were less than a hundred miles away from her. Mother would visit the old, familiar places, and she reunited with many old friends, all the time hoping to be able to make her way to Dr. Graham's Homes to see us.

I remember a very short visit from her, just a few hours really, when a friend was able to drive her up to Deolo Hill. Word reached me at the cottage that someone was asking for me, and I raced down the rough, stony path in my bare feet with the wings of a swift eagle, barely touching or noticing the ground beneath me. I came upon her standing by the three fir trees on the edge of a strip of grass just below the clock tower. I was about ten years old at the time, and I recognized her immediately even though I had been only four when I had seen her last. I stopped dead in my tracks. I lost my breath and I didn't know what to do. My feet would not move forward. I wanted to be in her arms the way I remembered, but time had dulled that feeling, and hugs were so far removed from my life by this time.

As she made her way to me, my eyes were riveted on her face. I glimpsed her smiling at me. Her beautiful, dark curls were caught up behind her head, and she had on a striped, purple and white frock, which billowed slightly in the gentle breeze. I remember every detail of her standing there as if it was yesterday, and I truly thought this was just a dream. When she spoke my name softly, I went to her and received a soft kiss on the cheek. I was in heaven.

She handed me a small bag of sweets and told me she could only stay a short while. Dr. Graham's Homes was restricted to all visitors, and anyone wanting access into the area could only do so with special written permission. My mother had no documents allowing her in. The visit was arranged at a moment's notice, as her friend was making a delivery to a client in Kalimpong, the town below Dr. Graham's Homes.

I knew my mother would have to leave again, and soon, as she mentioned not being allowed to visit us. I was the only one of her children lucky enough to see her during this visit, since my cottage was the closest to the school grounds where she was waiting. I didn't speak more than one or two words to her. There was too much to say and I didn't know how to start. Being painfully shy for most of my life, I would be flushed with the effort of just trying to get my words out. As I held her hand and gazed at her, I hoped that my eyes were telling her all she needed to know. I loved her to distraction, and I wanted to go away with her. She left me so very lonely and sad. I brought my hand up to my face and inhaled the slight fragrance of flowers that she left behind, just like the little blue forget-me-nots on the white handkerchief that she held. I ate my sweets slowly, saving three for my brothers, whom I would see later in the afternoon and would tell of her visit. I would treasure this memory of our mother's visit for many years to come and still do today, especially as it would be several more years before I would see her again.

Mother moved on, eventually finding her independence on her own and providing a home for us many years later. When she retired from her last job at Dow Hill School, I was already living in America. She wrote that she wanted to leave India and asked if I would help her immigrate. I was glad to do it and wanted nothing more. My husband at the time, along with my daughter who was seven, provided a home for her where she lived with us for a little more than twenty years.

She left behind my two younger brothers and our sister Sandra, the youngest, who was doing well on her own. I know she missed them terribly and wrote long letters to them constantly. She visited her three sons in England a couple of times, and they traveled over to the States to see her.

My efforts to teach her how to drive produced drastic results, so I signed her up for classes. My poor husband was the proud owner of his first Jeep, and between my mother and I we managed to make good use of the ditches surrounding our route. But through it all, he never complained. For all he knew, women from India had to be indulged at all times! He never knew if the Nepalese tirade that would burst forth from her was for him or his Jeep. Suffice it to say, the driving instructor loved Mary and the way she drove. The two of them would drive down Indian River Drive, scattering birds and palm tree fronds in their wake. My mother would come back from her lesson exhilarated and happy. I didn't want to be in the same vehicle as her. She seemed to have no fear and thought that everyone should be getting out of her way. I helped her with the road signs and questions in the book but left the actual driving test to the instructor.

My mother failed her test the first time, not for the obvious reasons, but because she didn't react to the ambulance bellowing its horn behind her. She succeeded on her second attempt. I struggled with letting her drive on her own, but she had more confidence in her abilities than I did, and the few short excursions we took turned up no incidents, or accidents.

Mum was extremely healthy, playing tennis and walking every day, swimming when she could, and learning to fish, which turned out to be one of her favorite things to do. She loved to cook the classic Indian curries she learned from Mrs. Mahbuk, and we enjoyed every one of the dishes put before us. I learned from her as well, and although Indian cooking can be a daunting and long process, the effort is worth the looks of joy the family gets when we get together and put on a feast.

Sadly, we found out on Mother's first visit to a doctor in the United States that her blood pressure was very high and somewhat unstable. She was put on medication and a salt-free diet. Mother struggled with this and, even after many warnings and much cajoling on my part she treated medication like it was the devil itself. More often than not, she would conveniently forget to take it. She would go from having a slight stroke to a severe one and eventually succumbed to pneumonia.

A few of my brothers and some of their children visited her here, and we all had a wonderful reunion, talking of good times and happier days. Towards the end of her life, Mother reverted back to speaking only Nepalese, and Ivan would carry the conversation for us, eliciting a smile and a giggle from her once in a great while. She passed away at the age of ninety in 2001, right after their visit and a year after her first stroke.

Ivan; his eldest son, Sean; and I made a trip to India the next year, carrying her ashes back to Kurseong, one of the happiest places she had known and where my sister also resides now. We chose a day to pack a picnic lunch of curry and rice in her honor and took a trip down the mountain to the place known as the Ballisands. It was here we scattered her ashes, at the place where the Rangeet and Ballisands Rivers meander down from the Himalayas and meet to form one. The area is breathtakingly beautiful. It was peaceful and alive, with rare, flitting butterflies and birds in full, sweet song. We floated garlands of marigolds and sweet jasmine (her fragrance) over the sparkling waters of the rivers and laid her to rest in the place we all knew she loved best. Fortunately, the customs authorities in India at every airport and customs station were quite helpful and respectful of our little urn, which we carried by hand to its final earthly home. We were given special consideration, which allowed us to take our mother home, without questions or searching or having to explain anything.

I often pondered one question over and over again: How was my father able to leave Mum and us so willingly? When I asked our mother the question years later, she tried to explain to me that it was not because of his children that he left. She explained that she lacked family support and funds to follow him when he found a new future with someone else who, unlike herself, had a strong family of her own. Oscar's friends in Siliguri and surrounding areas rallied around my mother and her children, and he would never be welcome there again.

I also wondered if, faced with my mother's circumstances at the time, could I, or would I, have given up all my children? That is a difficult question to answer. I am confident she thought only of what was best for us. She chose the only option open to her.

Chapter 3

It was Ivan's best paper kite. I had just put my hand through it, destroying it beyond repair. I remember thinking that I could not have done anything worse to incur his wrath, and I was in for a screaming tirade or even a cuff across my ear. He was six years older, and I knew that I would wither under his anger for having even touched the kite. To my surprise and joy, my petrified look and feelings of shame at what I had done were met with a calm look in his eyes and, eventually, a smile to follow. In the silence that ensued, he took me by the hand and led me away from the scene of the crime. With the torn kite in hand, he informed me that I was a little girl and didn't know about kites yet, but I was going to learn, and never again would I destroy a precious possession.

This was the earliest meaningful memory I have of Ivan. In the days to come and the difficult years ahead, he would forever be my guiding light and remains so now. With his encouragement and the gifts that God bestowed on him, Ivan would become a surrogate father to his younger siblings. He would help us through the difficult, crucial years of our life in the Homes without our parents. Ivan was truly admired and loved by nearly all who met him, for he was loyal to a fault and the first to lend a helping hand, going out of his way to make someone else's path easier. He was liked by the cottage and school staff and would make lasting friendships with some of them.

Ivan speaks of his early childhood years in Dr. Graham's Homes with fondness, and even though he had his share of punishments, the good outweighed the bad feelings. At times, his life was idyllic. He talks about the numerous camping trips to exotic places like Melli, Naziok, Rinkingpong, and Rilli, to name just a few. The boys were always given a certain amount of freedom and allowed to be on their own from time to time. How he loved to wander with his brothers and friends, chasing butterflies and gathering things to eat along the way.

Though we didn't have much time to seek each other out during the school week, he would nevertheless wait for me after the Sunday church service, along with my other brothers, where I would look at his flashing smile and soft, hazel eyes and cling to every word he spoke. These moments were, and still are, a backdrop in my mind, seeming to hang there permanently like a brightly lit curtain. Being a child of great imagination, I was always seeking an escape from sadness and loneliness. By using this curtain of joyous meetings with my brothers, I didn't have to go far into my scattered brain to be uplifted from dark days and lonely nights, especially in my youth.

Ivan was a budding artist and collected butterflies and stamps. His collections are fascinating to look at, and every rare stamp and butterfly had a story he loved to tell. My favorite was of the *Teinopalpus imperialis*, a rare and spectacular species of butterfly, found only in the forests surrounding Bhutan and Gangtok in the foothills of the Himalayas. The female is much larger than the male and carries six-inch long swallowtails on her lower wings. Their colors of purple, shimmering green, and gold help camouflage them high in the tree tops, where the species only hovers around towering trees that flower for a short period of time. They can be spotted, but very rarely did anyone have a chance to net one of them. During the British Rule of India, the butterflies were much coveted and could bring in any asking price from the seller.

On a hot summer day, an early morning walk to the Teesta River might lead to a rare sighting of the butterfly, pausing ever so fleetingly to light on a cool, shady puddle of dewy water to sip the delicious moisture. Before the observer's mind could grasp what his eyes were seeing, the elusive beauty would be soaring toward the high treetops and the bright sunlight above. Our father, who was also a lepidopterist, was lucky enough to have had a male species of the rare butterfly, having either bartered or traded for it, or been given one as a gift. But as usual, Oscar was not forthcoming with how he obtained it, and the truth of its existence in his collection is still a mystery. My brother has painted the butterfly numerous times with loving strokes of his colored pens, not leaving a single detail out. I love looking at it, but both my brother and myself would much rather have seen it free and on the wing, back in the hills of our home.

In letters written to me over the years, Ivan mentions the absence of our parents, but he had learned to deal with our early years much better than the rest of us, quite possibly because he had our mother and father present in his very early years much longer than most of us did. He remembers seeing our father only once after our entrance to Dr. Graham's Homes, and that was probably the same occasion I remember when he appeared long enough to have his picture taken with me and when he said his good-bye never to return. Ivan must have been fifteen at the time, but he mentions seeing our father once more, a couple of years later before our father left India for good.

That last meeting took place in Calcutta at the end of a month's vacation for my brother and three other boys from Hart Cottage. They had been staying at the Birkmyre Hostel in Calcutta, and while they were waiting at Sealdah train station for the return trip back to school, which would have been my brother's last year, Oscar appeared out of nowhere and whisked him away from the train platform. Ivan was bundled into a dark green Pontiac and found himself seated beside his father, traveling rather fast farther and farther away from his friends back at the station.

He soon found out that their destination was Siliguri again, which was familiar territory. The journey, which involved loading the car onto a ferry and traveling all night on the river, took two and a half days, and my brother was overjoyed at the newfound freedom and the sight of his father next to him. They finally rolled into Siliguri, and there, true to his nature, Oscar left my brother at the doorstep of Mrs. Mahbuk and our mother, who had been living there recently, probably waiting for Oscar's return.

Our father went on the final lap of the journey without Ivan, promising to return and take care of things. He returned after a week or so but left on some pretext, convincing my mother, as he always did, that he would be back. None of us saw him again until we immigrated to England several years later.

This chain of events led to dire circumstances for our mother, because at the same time young Rick, my second brother, had just arrived a few weeks prior, having run away after an incident had occurred back at Dr. Graham's Homes in regards to Jubilee House. So, here was my mother, without a job and with two young teenage boys on her hands (one seventeen and the other fifteen) and no money to support any of them. Mrs. Mahbuk came through again in her kindly way, and the three stranded souls were able to barely survive.

The boys lived those days wandering around Siliguri or trekking into the jungle of Sevoke, known for its man-eating tigers and leopards, with just a slingshot and a butterfly net. They would hunt for things to eat and would be gone until dark. My mother, at her wits end and concerned for her two children, appealed to Dr. Graham's Homes again. By now there was no kind person in the form of Mr. Purdee and no Daddy Graham to come to her aid. Ivan had missed his first day of the new school year, and in essence, my brothers were now runaways, for that is how the principal of the school viewed these latest events, and the boys were not accepted back into Dr. Grahams Homes.

My mother received a letter back from the principal in charge of the Homes, in which he stated that, although her boys could not return, there was an alternative solution. She would have to make a choice. Dr. Graham's Homes offered to send Ivan and Rick to a reform school deep in the jungles of northern India, bordering on the state of Assam. She in turn was offered a job interview with an Indian couple in Calcutta, which she was glad to accept, and made her own way down on the train, traveling third class. She was hired as a governess for the couple's young daughter, and her duties included teaching their child how to speak English. She would travel extensively with this family all over the world, but even though the opportunity arose for her to stay gone, she had only one thought on her mind. Her children would be her beacon, leading her back to India, and she knew that, one day soon, she would have them back.

Not knowing much on the subject of a reform school, Mother reluctantly agreed to have her sons taken from her once again. For some reason, Rick was sent ahead first, and Ivan followed a couple of months later. My brothers spent the rest of their teenage years cut off from everything and everyone they knew, and I felt that I had lost them forever. If Dr. Graham's Homes had been strict with discipline and confinement, Tanikpur, according to Ivan, was a dismal, lonely, mosquito-infested black hole, riddled with venomous snakes. The midday heat could make you feel as if you were being roasted alive. He could actually feel his skin sizzling in the heat as the sweat poured out of him. The students lived in a makeshift hut, with no doors, allowing the huge scorpions and other undesirable crawling things to make themselves at home. The beds were about six inches off the floor on four posts and made from rough coconut fibers. Mosquito netting was unheard of, and both boys contracted the dreaded malaria, which still lurks in their bodies and surfaces from time to time. The absence of a doctor and hospital made life precarious for the young teens living there, and in the case of the ones stricken with malaria, their care came down to quinine tablets and the tender loving care of a kind friend. Both Rick and Ivan were lucky to have had both these commodities, and these, along with their youth and strength of will, enabled them to survive. Wild animals prowled about at night, sometimes getting lucky enough to bag their prey, and the boys who could would scamper up a banyan tree and stay there until dawn.

In charge of the mission was a Mr. Small, and he started out being a good, decent man. He had brought his family along from America and ran a self-contained, little community. But by the time both my brothers left, Mr. Small had become a different person, treating males roughly and maintaining prison-like control over them and taking the females for his own pleasures and pursuits. Ivan got away as soon as he could or was allowed to, but Rick, who was only fifteen when he first arrived at the farm, found the shooting forays and farming with American heavy machinery much to his liking and stayed on for several years, learning all he could, until he too became disillusioned with the lifestyle of Mr. Small.

When Ivan left Tanikpur, he made his way back to the only place he knew he would find acquaintances and, perhaps, some friends, his footsteps leading him back to Siliguri and Kalimpong. As luck would have it, one of his traveling companions on the train was a former acquaintance and ex-Homes' boy just like he was. This companion was the son of a Mr. George Mace, a prominent member of the community of Kalimpong and surrounding towns. Mr. Mace also happened to be a good friend of our father, now gone from India. On hearing my brother's story, his traveling companion, whose name was George, suggested they both travel on together to his father's home in Kalimpong, where help would be waiting.

Mr. Mace, who was Nepalese, had a large family of nine children, some of them being around the same age as my brother and who were also ex-Homes boys and girls.

Mr. Mace was the chief operator and supervisor of the Rong Gong Cinchona Plantation, located on the outskirts of Kalimpong. The plantation produced, among other things, quinine from the bark of the massive Cinchona trees. Here again, a member of our family would be rescued by a prominent, caring human being from the state of Nepal. Just as Mr. Mahbuk from Siliguri had done, Mr. Mace would welcome my brother into the family, inviting him to move into their large bungalow, where he stayed until Mr. Mace found him a very good job after a month or so. My brother became an apprentice driller on the Jaldaka Hydro Electric Water Project, which provided much needed, precious water to places like Siliguri and the surrounding towns, as well as to the large tea estates in the remote area of the Duaars. With his genial personality and quick mind, my brother soon mastered the drills, studying all aspects of the workings of the handheld electric machinery.

Here in Jaldaka, his likable personality and sunny nature led to some great friendships, with both the supervisor in charge and the local Nepalese folk who worked alongside him. By now, he spoke their language fluently, and they laughed at all his antics and took his teasing as a way of life. On the long trips to Kalimpong, which Mr. Mace would take now and then to check in on his family, Ivan would go along for the ride, popping in to see Mum, who by this time had secured a post in Dr. Graham's Homes, having brought my baby sister with her. Ivan was paid well and was happy. He found this life and his friends quite suitable and to his liking, but knew all the time that it would not last.

Our father had decided, or maybe he was coerced, into sending for Ivan and Rick to make the trip to England and take up their lives there with him. Dr. Graham's Homes' secretary, along with the help of the UK high commissioner in Calcutta, helped with the important task of obtaining a British subject passport for both of them. Before long it was time for them to bid India good-bye.

Leaving wasn't easy for my brothers. After all, they were leaving everything that was familiar behind. Although the future in England sounded exciting, they were heartbroken at leaving their mother, friends, and siblings behind.

My brothers left in 1959. My mother's heart broke completely that year, and she went into a depression that she was never able to fully recover from.

Ivan lives in England now, and even though he loves his two sons and their children, his heart and soul is still in the hills of the Himalayas, as is mine. We reminisce every time we get together. Our stories are always about the days of camping, chasing butterflies, and flying kites so high we challenged the clouds. We speak Nepalese together, and he cooks all of my mother's and my favorite dishes. Thanks to his keeping every piece of memorabilia from all of us over the years, my visits across the ocean bring back nostalgia for the home we once knew in India and long for even now. The memories are always fresh and new again, and my dear mother, brothers, and sister come alive as if it was yesterday.

Chapter 4

I found myself, at almost five years old, facing a daunting set of stone steps that led up to a wooden veranda. Behind me was a small compound with a set of long, wire lines stretched between two wooden poles, which, I would learn later, was the clothesline. If you stepped behind these lines, you would be a foot away from a sheer drop that plunged suddenly down fifteen feet to a narrow dirt and grass path. This turned out to be a shortcut that circuited our large compound to the west side. It wound its way to the edge of the girl's playing field below us, continued behind the boy's facility past several buildings, and disappeared into the hillside above the school classrooms. The local cooks and their families used this hidden path to access the cottage kitchens and to carry their daily supplies back and forth to their homes located further down on the hillside. I later used these paths to find quiet places to hide when I needed to, which was often.

I stood quietly and slowly turned. I walked to the edge of the drop, and looking straight ahead at the immense vastness in front of me, I was frightened. In later years, I would come to love the deep valleys and woods, the faraway winding rivers, and the full Himalayan mountain range. But at the moment, it all seemed to be the end of the world. I was alone and afraid. I couldn't seem to remember having said good-bye to my mother, and I felt a strange rumbling in my tummy. The fear of being alone without my mother and brothers overwhelmed me, and I started to scream. I could not catch my breath. Or maybe I was just holding it. Either way, I could not make myself stop. I was running out of time and started walking in a tight, little circle, moving unconsciously closer toward the edge of the cliff.

I'm not sure how long I continued this way, but I finally realized that I was lying on the grass. I heard a voice. It was not a child's voice or my mother's but one that sounded strange. It was telling me that I must stop crying, and I should try to sit up.

I opened my tightly closed eyes, hoping to see a familiar face. Instead, I saw a circle of children's faces looking down at me where I lay. There was utter silence as I gazed up at them. Most of them had dark hair and eyes like my mother, but standing over them was a woman who had short, blond hair and fair skin like me. I was helped to my feet by this person, and at the same time, I heard a bell being rung. The rest of the children made a dash up the steps, and I was left with a stranger who was holding me by the hand. I was coaxed into following her up the steps and into the building, where she steered me toward a room full of talking and laughing children.

Some of the girls were bigger and towered over me, but a couple of them were smaller. I was led to the end of a bench that was attached to a long wooden table with a white tablecloth on it. The grown-up clapped her hands, and the noise immediately turned into silence. She introduced me as a new girl and said that my name was Yvonne.

At that point, I was on my own again. I faced inward, staring at the table in front of me when everyone started to sing with their eyes closed. The singing did not last very long, and soon they all slid onto the wooden benches to sit in front of a plate with a spoon and cup next to each one. I had one too, and as I gazed at the liquid in the plate and smelled the aroma of something that was alien to me, my mind searched again for anything familiar. I watched warily as everyone began spooning the liquid into her mouth in silence. The little girl next to me tore off a piece of brown bread and chewed it quickly. My hands were still in my lap. I was having difficulty swallowing and was not able to move any of the liquid from the plate to my mouth. I sat there with my eyes downcast until everyone stood up a few minutes later, and one voice said a short thank you to God. (I had some idea of who *he* was, because I distinctly remember my father thanking God many times.) At this time, I was told to remain seated and finish my dinner.

Needless to say, I was not able to get the spoon past my nose without gagging. I was not hungry, and this was not my mother's food. I made little balls of the dry, brown bread and moved them around on the plate. I was sitting all alone at the table now and felt less overwhelmed than I had at first. I cautiously raised my head to look around. I think I had begun to realize that my mother was not close by and that I was expected to do what everyone else was doing.

After what seemed like a very long time, the grown-up who had led me here came back into the large room and helped me swing my legs around the bench to stand facing her. I was still in my blue dress that my mother had dressed me in earlier, and I had a blue ribbon in my hair that tied up my blond curls. My shoes and socks were gone, and I couldn't remember what had happened to them. The voice talking to me now was quiet but not harsh. I was told to go with an older girl to the dressing room to get ready for bed. This would be the first and only time I would get away with not finishing my meal. Quite often, I would stand for hours by myself praying that the little round bread balls would slide down my throat without getting stuck. In weeks to come, I managed to flick the bread out through the window and onto the veranda, where the crows and sparrows would quietly make them disappear.

The washroom was a large, cold room, with three sinks and a stone washtub. I was given a toothbrush and a cake of red soap with which to wash my face and hands. My feet were washed in the bathtub, along with five other girls who were close to my age. We dried ourselves with white, cotton towels and hung them on a peg with our names written above. One of the girls helped me undress, and I put on a stiff, white, cotton gown that came down to my ankles.

Scrubbed and clean with shiny faces, we were marched in single file down the hall to a closed door. After the older girl knocked and was told to enter, we filed into a brightly lit room, where two grown-ups sat in front of a table. I glanced briefly at the white bread, butter, and biscuits in front of the grown-ups but didn't give it much thought other than to wonder if I might be hungry tomorrow since today I was not. The familiar grown-up spoke and asked if we were all ready for bed. She inspected hands and feet and reminded everyone to say her prayers. Then one by one, the little girls stepped forward and kissed both grown-ups on the cheek and said, "Good night, Aunty."

I was the last in line and still had not uttered a single word since screaming by the edge of the compound earlier in the evening.

I didn't step forward right away and was slightly pushed in the direction of the "aunty." When I approached and stood facing her, she leaned forward to kiss my cheek as she called my name and said good night. The other grown-up repeated the ritual, and we were all ushered out of the room.

I walked up some shiny, wooden stairs to a room with one overhead light and beds down each side of the long walls. The beds were all made up with red blankets and a pillow at the top, with just enough space for a small body to pass in between. As I stood staring, each girl seemed to know where her bed was and went straight to it. The girls all knelt down with their hands together on top of the blanket. I was led to the second bed from the entryway, but not having learned yet how to kneel and pray, I sat on my bed until I was told to turn back the blanket and get in. Each little girl's bed had an older girl's bed next to it, usually an older sister if they had one, or someone assigned as her charge if there was no sister available. The light was turned out. I lay in my bed and tried to see through the dark.

I was alone for the first time without my mother nearby, and though I was not afraid of the dark, I nevertheless felt the need for the familiar closeness I was used to. The sobs started, at first softly and then louder as I cried out for my loved ones. No amount of "shushing" could make me stop. When I realized my mother was not coming and with all the events of the day so far, I became very tired and sleepy. I put my thumb into my mouth— at least that was familiar—and gradually, the sobs faded away. The tears dried on my cheeks, and I fell asleep on my first night without my family.

Birissa Cottage was one of about twenty-two cottages in 1947. At the young age of five, I learned to live and exist with thirty other children of all ages and nationalities. I did not see my parents again for ten years, until my mother came back in 1957. For the next fourteen years of my life, I grew up in a strong Christian environment in this small, sheltered community of Dr. Graham's Homes, in Kalimpong, India. Even though the sometimes harsh and lonely existence would try to overtake me, I learned to seek out my strengths and tried hard to overcome my weaknesses. I would meet people who were less than desirable, but I would also meet truly wonderful people who impacted my life along the way and to whom I will ever be grateful.

Chapter 5

As I gradually became more acquainted with my new life, my parents were constantly in my thoughts, and their images never faded away. I thought of my father as I had seen him last. He was at my bedside, and according to my mother, I had come down with yellow fever. I could still picture him holding me in his arms as he helped me open a large box he had brought for me. The beautiful doll inside became my constant companion as I lay in bed, and I could still smell the fragrance of her skin and hair. I had no other picture in my head of my father at the time and can't remember seeing him after my illness, but I was happy with my memories of him smiling down at me when I curled up inside my strange new bed. I constantly heard the voice of my mother calling me and clung to the image of her holding me as I peered down at my baby brother, Julian, sleeping in his basket beside her bed. Her sweet face would be close to mine, and I would play with her long black hair, so unlike mine, and we would laugh at my brother's attempts to catch his rattle. I missed my parents terribly. I had no idea it would be years before I would see either of them again.

I soon realized there were both boys' and girls' cottages. They were all alike, and each one had its own name and color to identify it from the others. I lived in Birissa Cottage, and our assigned color was red. Sometimes it was hard to find red fabric, so more often than not, we made do with hot pink, or even orange, which most of us detested. My brothers, Ivan, Rick, Mitchell, and Ashton, all belonged to Hart Cottage, and their color was light blue. Siblings were always assigned to the same cottage. My brothers were fortunate they had each other while on the other hand, I was alone. Most of the cottages were named after British or Scottish cities or viceroys to India. My cottage, however, was named for two sister cities in central India, Bihar and Orissa. The citizens of these two cities, many of them British, donated enough money in 1915 to build the much-needed cottage to house the growing number of homeless children.

Dr. Graham's Homes was originally founded as a home for abandoned and orphaned Anglo Indian children. More space was eventually needed to accommodate the rising admissions, and without funds, Daddy Graham had to come up with new and innovative ideas to generate the much-needed cash. In order to keep its head above water, the Kalimpong Committee allowed Dr. Graham's Homes to take in paying day scholars as well. Some of the parents who could afford tuition would pay according to their financial status, thereby adding to the school's income.

By the time my brothers and I arrived, the great pioneers and visionaries who founded Dr. Graham's Homes were no longer alive. With them went some of the most wonderful and caring human beings on the face of the earth. Daddy Graham; his wife, Kathryn; Mr. Purdee; and countless missionaries who gave up their own homes to care for these needy children were irreplaceable. With the increase in the number of children pouring in and the individual care needed for them, the difficult task of being compassionate and loving caregivers was an immense challenge, and discipline and demand for total compliance sometimes took precedence.

The first housemother in my new life in Birissa Cottage was a missionary by the name of Miss Cavington, whose permanent home was in Australia. All cottage housemothers were addressed as Aunty by the children. This aunty would influence my young life for about five years, after which she returned home on furlough, and someone else replaced her. Unless circumstances warranted, like sickness, family death, or marriage, most housemothers signed a two-, three-, or five-year contract. After their contract was over they would return to their own countries. Some would not return, but others did come back after staying away a year or two.

Under the current aunty, I was led firmly down the path of obedience and discipline. I became acquainted with the rules quickly, so I would not have to come face-to-face with the back of a wooden hairbrush. This was a very unpleasant form of punishment for me, and no matter what, I could not totally avoid it. I found it impossible to get through my childhood unscathed. My first experience with the dreaded brush came very early in my second month. It involved my brother Mitchell, who was older than me by about a year and a half. Not only did I experience pain and shame, but I caused him to go through it as well.

Food, for the most part, was healthy, although lacking in variety and flavor. I was either not eating enough or eating too much of the wrong things when the opportunity arose. On one particular day, we were given two slices of white bread that had been buttered with margarine. While I ate one piece and found it to my liking, I made the decision to save the other slice for my brother, so I hid it under my pinafore that covered my work overall. The girl next to me watched this take place but never said a word to anyone at the time. It was a Saturday morning, and I knew I would see my brother later in the afternoon, as brothers were allowed to visit sisters in their cottages on this day.

When my brother showed up, we both disappeared behind the washhouse, out of sight to anyone. I shyly presented him with the slice of bread, which was a bit hard but still intact. We sat in a makeshift shelter of old scraps of cloth and burlap I had constructed on a carpet of dried ferns I had gathered earlier. My brother had every intention of breaking the bread in two so we could each have a piece. It never came to that, for in the next instant, the aunty came around the corner of the building and found our hiding place. I knew I was in trouble. I felt that I deserved the punishment for hiding food, but I was not prepared to hear her accuse me of stealing it. We both followed her around the washhouse and into the cottage, straight past the girl who had seen me hide the bread. She only looked away as I walked by. We came to a stop in the staff sitting room. My brother was first to be punished. One of the hardest things I have ever experienced was watching my brother get punished for something I did. I counted the loud smacks and cried in anger and frustration. I tried to convince the aunty that the bread was from my own dinner. Unlike him, I cried at every stroke I was dealt. In later years, as I grew older, the tears would dry up and become nonexistent for me. A confrontation with the other girl would have led to more punishment, but there was no rule against choosing your own playmates, and for a while, avoidance was the only way out for me.

This incident led to many others like it, where I would be accused of stealing. I began to feel guilty, although I never actually committed the crime. I became more distrustful of everyone and shied away from contact with most people. I spoke only when spoken to and answered with one-syllable words. It wasn't long before I began processing my thoughts differently, and all too often, I invited more disciplinary action against myself. I understood now how one little incident could grow over the years and seem to become more and more difficult to overcome.

I spent my first two years attending kindergarten. I learned well and loved reciting poetry. I spoke with a lisp and was called on more often than I can remember to recite the poem "Waves," complete with actions and expressions. I was glad when I grew too old for all of that. I learned to sing hymns and memorized Bible verses, sometimes winning competitions, along with Ashton, who was better than all of us put together. I liked my teachers and didn't mind going to school. I preferred going to school instead of doing housework and learned to like other girls who were not in my cottage. I played Dick Whittington's wife in the play *Puss in Boots*, where I had to change my costume seven times at six years old. But I didn't have to speak a word, and that was perfect for me.

This particular housemother and her five-year rule of Birissa left me more morose, and I withdrew to the other side of my wall and stayed there. There was no progress made in my cottage life, and my report cards would state that there was nothing to report. I just needed to do better. My report cards never went anywhere and were put away for the next aunty to look over. One time, I was accused of stealing some plum jam from the staff table set for afternoon tea. The harder I tried to convince them all that I was nowhere near the plum jam but knew who was, the more I received humiliating treatment. One older girl went so far as to borrow a raw egg from the aunty, which she floated in a basin of water. If the egg sank, it would prove I was guilty. Well of course it did, and that sealed my fate. Not only did I get punished with the back of the brush, which was degrading enough, but from that moment on, whenever something came up missing, I would immediately be the guilty one. My "crime" would be punishable by extra dirty drains for me to scrub.

The Christmas holidays during these years were extra gloomy, and it was hard to find joy in an unfriendly and dull environment. When I was ten years old, I looked for ways to lift my spirits on my own. On the good days, when I was not being punished, I would scramble quickly out of my gray overalls, making sure I put them away, and run down the stone steps in the sunshine to the playing field of the school compound to search for my brothers. I could usually find Mitchell, and sometimes Ashton, and we would roam the hillsides in our bare feet looking for wild raspberries and cherries. I would laugh in the company of my brothers and enjoyed watching their antics. We found one old rusty roller skate, and I remember Mitchell falling off the edge of the veranda into the prized flower beds, unable to stop due to the lack of any brakes.

Sometimes we would wander farther and wind up unexpectedly at a small clearing with a neat, makeshift thatched hut and meet some of the local Nepalese people. At times, there would be children around, and a staring contest would begin. We looked strange to them, and they in turn spoke no English. In the small patches of earth, there would be mounds of corn ready to be ground or little piles of green, prickly squash; white sweet potatoes; huge cucumbers, and even a small grove of pomelo trees.

One element of my early childhood that I would never forget was hunger. It was with great joy that we accepted some corn on the cob from the villagers who took pity on us as we looked on with huge, hungry eyes. Our three meals a day consisted mainly of oatmeal, rice, potatoes, and bread, which were a welcome sight as the hunger pains set in. It was my own fault that I could not eat the boiled potatoes and force down the brown bread, so I constantly looked for wild things to eat and wound up with a stomachache more often than not.

Eventually, Miss Cavington returned to her home in Australia and I can't recall ever having seen her again. My first five years at Dr. Graham's Homes did nothing to endear me to life in the cottage. I found those years to be difficult. I hadn't adjusted well to the harsh authority of my elders, who seemed to have no kindness in their hearts, and to the discipline they dealt out. Defiance and aloofness did not help my situation, and I was not capable of looking into the future to see the brighter days ahead. I felt doomed to this life of loneliness and bleak existence. I had not seen or heard from my parents in all these years. Even so, I still held onto the hope of seeing my mother very soon. It was only a matter of when that day would come.

➤··➤

Caning of boys was still carried out in our early years at The Homes, and my brothers did not escape any of it. Once, Mitchell and some other boys his age wanted to escape the confines of cottage life and decided they would run away to see how far they could go without being caught. They made it as far as the Teesta Bridge, thirty miles away, on foot. They were caught by the patrol officer in charge of the bridge.

Children from Dr Graham's Homes were well identified by their school uniforms, bare feet, and lighter complexions, along with their speaking English and always being hungry. A call was made to the headmaster, who sent the school Land Rover to help bring the children back.

It wasn't until the boys were already well underway when Mitchell discovered that Ashton had snuck in at the back of the group. Mitchell was not overjoyed to see his little brother, but it was too late to do anything about it. Ashton kept pace with the older runaways, and when it came time for the officer in charge to round up the boys, Ashton could not be found. As the officer tried to catch up with the little escapee, who was small and quick, the rest of the boys would tumble back out of the vehicle and would have to be captured again. This cat and mouse game went on for some time. Since my brother was so small, he could hide in the tiniest hole, making it difficult to be spotted.

The runaways were eventually caught and driven back to Dr. Graham's Homes, where they were paraded in front of everyone. Needless to say, they were caned in the headmaster's office, although Ashton, being so small, got away with very little discipline.

In the meantime, life in Birissa Cottage did not change much from day to day. I was eleven years old now, and I remember this time as being particularly difficult for me. I was past the age of requiring help with everything and had to get along on my own. I did everything methodically. I disliked cottage life and the harsh work that went with it, so I honed my skills in getting away with anything I could. I answered back in a sullen way to any situation involving authority by an adult or older girl and paid the consequences of either the back of a hand or the wooden hairbrush. I had few friends in the cottage and used my fists to make my point, not realizing that this was not an answer to my frustrations. There had been no contact with my parents, and my older brothers seemed to be in the spotlight constantly for some infraction or another.

It didn't help that the next housemother to arrive in the cottage was known for the forceful way she dealt with girls who were reluctant to bend to her authority. I was smart enough to know that life would be easier for me if I were to work my way into her good graces, and I did try at first. But it wasn't long before my attempts became futile, as her favorites were mostly my enemies. I could not pretend to get along with someone I disliked, and being gracious to that person was one of the most difficult skills for me to develop. Therefore, the aunty, or housemother as she was often referred to, was the highest priority on my list of people I needed to avoid at all costs.

It was an incident involving two older boys that took over the whole school's conversation, creeping into all our minds and staying there for months to come. Two boys between the ages of seventeen and eighteen were caught bullying the smaller boys in their cottage. We filed into Jarvie Hall, taking our places and whispering to each other about why we were all gathered there. It wasn't long before the headmaster came out on stage and stood in front of the podium. He seemed very solemn and spoke in a slow, measured voice. I don't remember much of what he said, but soon he was calling the two older boys up on onto the stage to stand on either side of the podium. Events happened rapidly after that. The boys were both caned. Neither uttered a sound, but as I watched their faces redden and crumple silently, I shrank away and hid my eyes. All I could think about was that I wanted to talk to my brothers. I had to know they were not the ones who had been bullied. I knew that neither of the two boys belonged to Hart Cottage, so hopefully my brothers were safe. A public flogging had taken place, and I never experienced the likes of it again; nor did I want to.

At this time, I remember an incident when I had to stand in my underwear, at breakfast, in front of thirty girls, because I had failed to put my folded overall away in my locker. I don't think it helped that some of the anger and resentment I had built up over the years used to manifest itself in the way I looked at people. Not being encouraged to speak out, I could not translate my feelings, for fear of being insubordinate, so I was learning to hold my anger and loneliness close to me.

The physical punishment came to an abrupt end when I threatened to run away. Being twelve years old, I felt that, if my brothers could do it, so could I. I think the aunty knew by now, that I was willing to take desperate measures, which in turn would reflect upon her ability as a housemother. All subsequent disobedience and infractions of the rules were punishable by extra work duties and detentions. I became immune to all of it. I certainly was not the only one running into trouble. I just seemed to be doing more of it. At least it seemed that way to me.

One particular winter, in my preteen years, I spent the Christmas holidays alone with a few of the girls who were also without a home to go to. On a cold, dark afternoon, I had a chance encounter with the *chowkidhar* (night watchman). He was sitting alone with two of his children, around a hot coal fire in the washhouse of the cottage. As usual, I was wandering around on my own and was invited to sit and warm myself. I sat on my haunches just like the other children did and watched with huge, hungry eyes as whole ears of corn were produced and neatly sliced off the cob by the chowkidhar's kukri (Nepalese hunting knife) and put into a hot *kerahi* (wok), which was sitting on the fire. I can still smell the delicious aroma of the hot corn popping into big, soft, white puffs. I was allowed to have an equal share as the others. I could not have wished for anything better than being there in that moment, listening to the sweet Nepalese chatter, feeling warm as toast, and eating the most delicious food I had ever tasted. When my mind wanders today and I think of Dr. Graham's Homes, it is times like these that are upmost in my memories.

In my early teens, I was given the opportunity to choose dance as one of my after school activities. We had a lovely Anglo Indian music teacher. I not only learned the basics of ballet positions, I also incorporated the graceful movements into everything I did. I walked about stepping with my toes first and my back stiff as a board. My classmates just rolled their eyes, knowing I was apt to try new and strange things.

The lessons in ballet led me to join up with my Indian friends at school, and they in turn, taught me the classical hand gestures and movements of some of the timeless, beautiful dances of their culture. Together we would turn out plays and pantomimes that drew crowds from as far away as Calcutta.

I had found a true love in our little theatre. I could put on a good performance, as long as I could dance or act. But I wanted nothing to do with speaking lines. I was learning that I could escape into a different world whenever I allowed myself to, and the results were truly gratifying. I found what I loved to do best, like dancing, storytelling, and even writing. And my spirits lifted as my flights of fancy soared. I could endure anything, while I waited for my mother's return.

Chapter 6

A typical day for me started at six o'clock every morning. I jumped out of bed, said a quick prayer on my knees by the bedside, dressed in my overalls, and made my bed as neatly as I could. The four- and five-year-olds were helped by an older charge or, in some cases, an older sister if they had one. After a quick wash, I stood with everyone else at the breakfast table by 6:15 a.m., where the blessing was sung before we sat down. This first meal consisted of porridge; mostly oatmeal, which we ate without sugar, two slices of brown bread; a piece of fruit, mostly bananas; and a cup of tea. I eventually became accustomed to moving aside the floating bugs in our cereal and pushing them to the rim of the plate. Our cups of tea were flavored with salt, as sugar was scarce. A hymn or two was sung, and a prayer was conducted by the housemother after breakfast, whereby we were dismissed to get started on our particular duty for the day.

Chores started right after breakfast at 6:30 a.m. Included in our daily routines were some daunting tasks. For most of us, cleaning, washing and scrubbing, soon became just another part of our daily lives. The cottage was totally maintained and kept up to par by the children themselves, leaving only meals to be prepared by a cook from the local area. Even the little ones were taught to walk around the compound picking up dead fallen leaves or other debris, which they carried in their pinafores to the dustbin by the side of the washhouse. A senior girl, with the help of a younger protégé, washed and dried thirty sets of dishes, cups, and silverware in a stone scullery, after which everything was stacked on shelves, ready for the dining room duo to set the tables for the next meal. Kitchen duties, again with a senior/junior duo, consisted of carrying coal from the "go down" back to the kitchen, keeping the fire stoked in the grate, and lifting the ashes all through the day. The solid, wooden cooking tables were scoured with rough salt, baking soda, and a scrub brush, and left to dry until the next meal was prepared. The wooden kitchen floor was hand polished and rubbed to reveal its glowing boards.

Scrubbing the washroom floor was also a chore assigned to an older girl and her helper. It was this pair's duty to organize bath routines for everyone. There was no running hot water, so a fire had to be lit downstairs, conducting heat through pipes to the large holding tank upstairs. Bathing took place every other day during school days. Bathing thirty children in the space of one hour, while they all had cleaning duties to perform, was a feat I still marvel at today. This was accomplished in groups, with the four- to six-year-olds going first. Each group could use just one aluminum tub of water for about ten of them. A fresh tub was used for the next group of seven- to ten-year-olds, and then another one for the eleven- to fifteen-year-olds. Lastly, the older ones would have to make do in whatever way they could, hoping there was some hot water left for them at the end. I used to think it would have been better if older girls bathed on alternate days, allowing for more time for each, but obviously an expensive coal fire everyday was out of the question.

There were no classes to attend on anatomy or any other bodily functions, and we were left to discover on our own the new changes taking place in us. It was impossible for everyone to have fresh, clean clothes every day, as washing was collected only once a week. While we made do with what was available in our younger years, I discovered as I got older that washing my own by hand every day was a necessity. As our bodies changed and matured, the lack of privacy did little to alleviate the strain of not only dealing with the changes taking place in our bodies, but also overcoming the embarrassment of what was happening to us. Of course there was curiosity in our differences, but no one spoke a word, not allowing for any discussion to take place. Fortunately for me, a shower was installed in my seventeenth and eighteenth year, allowing a few of us the privacy we all craved. This was a huge relief, as the dreaded bath day became something I looked forward to and enjoyed and something I would never, ever take for granted.

Dining room duties for the seniors consisted of setting the large, wooden tables three times a day, making sure everyone was on time for meals, removing the used utensils to the scullery, and polishing the floor of the large room twice a day. The hallway, stairs, and upper landing where most of the traffic was concentrated, became the responsibility of an older girl as well. She hand polished the wooden floors and banisters, rubbing first against the grain and then with it to achieve a glass-like finish. This area was always the first sight a visitor would encounter, so it was very important that it was left perfect every morning. The aunty supervised the making of our own wax, with which we polished all the beautiful hardwood floors. Turpentine, the main ingredient, was mixed with liquid soap and a white wax and heated to a very high temperature. It would harden when cooled and would be applied by hand.

One of the senior girls would have the duty of supervisor of the staff pantry. She would help the cook prepare the staff meals and also learned how to set a table with fine china and crockery. This took place three to four times a day. It was her responsibility to serve the staff meals, wait on them, and clean everything up when the last dish of dessert was presented and eaten. It was during pantry duty that I learned how to make a perfect cup of tea and serve it in the most proper of English ways.

The staff meals were served at a separate table. Their food was prepared by the Nepalese cook, who made it a point to cater to their individual pallets. Sometimes, pantry duty could be the most coveted of all the jobs, due to leftovers that remained after the late evening meal was served. The pantry girls could be lucky enough to get some leftover Indian curry and rice or a delectable chop seasoned just right. Sometimes, there would even be enough to share with a friend. The one drawback with this particular duty, though, was that, more often than not, the girl on pantry duty would still be up washing and scrubbing after everyone else was relaxing and getting ready for bed.

Two girls in the intermediate age group took on the responsibilities of scrubbing toilets, polishing silver, dusting staff rooms, and keeping the girl's locker room in order. A younger child would be responsible for delivering and retrieving the mail twice a day. Some cottages were further away than others from the post office allowing for some long trips back and forth. A junior would be assigned to a senior so she, too, could learn the routines and how to go about getting things done. I can't remember whether I had a favorite duty I liked to perform. They all just became a routine part of my life that was necessary to exist from day to day.

Some duties were easier to perform than others. Therefore, monthly rotations were a necessity. There was little time to accomplish all the tasks we needed to in our short time frame every day, as the demand for perfection was sometimes extreme. Everything had to be inspected by the housemother, and until she gave her permission, no one could begin the next step, which was getting ready for school. By about 7:30 a.m., everyone was washing or bathing, if it was bath day. There was no makeup or curling irons. There was only one mirror and one dressing room for thirty girls to share. The older girls would also have a small charge to get ready for school. We not only succeeded in getting it all done, but also did it five days a week for fourteen years or more.

Our summer school uniforms consisted of a square-necked, royal blue tunic, belted at the waist and worn over a button-up shirt with a collar and short sleeves. It was either red or hot pink to represent Birissa cottage. The boys' summer attire consisted of khaki shorts and button-up, short-sleeve shirts. Laundry was sent out only once a week, and hand washing before bed became a necessity at the end of the day, especially since deodorant and other personal items were nonexistent at the time. When the aunties were satisfied that everything was in place, the school day began with a run down the hill and up again to the little chapel on the next rise, where the short service started at 8:15 a.m. Children were allowed to run in groups or individually, not waiting for the usual lineup of each cottage that was reserved for church on Sunday. Everyone had to be on his or her way to the chapel by 8:00 a.m., and the oldest girl would be the one to make sure everything was accomplished, sometimes making her late for the start of chapel herself.

School started promptly at 8:30 a.m., with a twenty-minute recess at 10:00 a.m. and a lunch at 11:30 a.m., which allowed us to scamper back to our cottages for the ever-looming cleanups that needed to be done. Between the ages of ten and sixteen, I became friends with a girl who had been crippled by polio. While we all went about barefoot, she was fitted with a special pair of shoes, one built up higher to allow for her weaker leg, making it difficult for her to walk. The shoe was heavy, and it took a lot of effort for her to make the long walk to and from chapel every day. I carried her on my back to and from school, and I remember us getting hysterical at some of the spills we took while negotiating the rough stone steps or steep climbs. Because the going was considerably slower for us, we were excused from chapel during school mornings. I hoped I didn't miss out on all the blessings and said my own little quick prayer on the way to school with my good friend on my back. She and I were also let out five minutes early at lunchtime so we could get a head start. We were a pair, one of us never without the other, and were seen everywhere as we made our way merrily to and from school every day. She was sent to a special hospital after awhile, and I missed her terribly. At the time, it seemed I was always parting from those I loved.

At 11:30 m., the gong would sound, and we would all race back to our cottages for the lunch break. We would have a meal of stew, made from pieces of meat (beef), potatoes, turnips, and carrots. The lunch was always the same and varied only on Christmas or Easter Sunday. We ate pork and chicken on those days. Seasoning was scarce, so we made do with lots of very hot chilies, which we grew behind the washhouse or got from the cook for helping him in the kitchen. Lunch always came with dessert—rice, tapioca, or bread pudding. This was our only real source of milk, apart from the cup of tea in the morning and evening. Dessert was usually something we looked forward to, especially since it was flavored with sugar. A glass of water was always served with lunch, but we were not allowed to drink a drop until we had eaten everything.

When lunch was over, we gave thanks to God and dressed in our overalls to begin cleaning the pots and pans and washing and scrubbing dishes and floors. Hands and faces were quickly washed, school uniforms donned again, and the school gong rung promptly at 1:00 p.m. for the afternoon session.

If there were any after-school activities scheduled, such as team sports, we wore a white gym shirt under our tunics instead of the colored shirt we normally wore. The gym shirt was a square-necked garment that had a place for a six-inch colored flag to be tied on the left shoulder. This flag represented the cottage to which you belonged. We also wore black bloomers under our tunics or carried them with us to put on just before the athletics began.

School let out at 3:30 p.m., and most of the children would then proceed either to the gym or the playing fields for hockey, net ball, soccer, or rounders. Track-and-field seasons were held after the monsoon months had passed, and by the end of October, all athletic events would be over. Swimming practice started in June, and the swimming gala was held at the end of August. Our swimsuits consisted of a dark blue, one-piece, braless costume, with straps on the shoulders and cut around the top of the leg. A cotton bonnet that tied under the chin, again in our cottage color for identification, would be worn every time we went into the pool. During the swimming races, it was easy to identify your favorite and cheer her on. The boys were not as easily identifiable as they did not wear bonnets, but wore their colors on the side of their swim shorts. Some of my fondest memories are of the swimming gala days, where over a thousand voices could be heard screaming for victory. All children had to participate, and all teaching staff took turns in organizing and refereeing.

Most of the children would return to the cottage for the 6:00 p.m. dinner bell. A bowl of hot soup with vegetables would be waiting, along with a couple of slices of brown bread and a cup of hot tea to go along with it. When in season, golden corn on the cob was a special treat, and though there was not a great deal of variety, I'm sure it was all nutritious. With the evening meal over, we sang hymns and were led in prayer by a senior girl.

Sometime during the year, we all had to learn the Lord's Prayer in Hindi and recite it every night. The pots, pans, and dishes had to be hastily washed again, the younger children readied for bed by six, and the senior girls prepared for night study at 6:30 p.m.

Night study, for seniors only, was supervised for two hours at the study hall on the school grounds. No uniform was required for this, so we wore clothing that was issued to us for leisure time. The middle and lower classes did their homework under housemother supervision for two hours in the cottage dining room. These two hours were carried out under the strictest of conditions. You were expected to work on homework and nothing else and could not be caught reading any other book except the one issued in your specific class.

Until my last two years in Dr. Graham's Homes, I cared little for study hall and found it dull and boring. Reading school-issued books held nothing for me, especially as I had read them over and over. I started looking for other things to read, in a variety of subjects, sneaking them in under a brown cover. I was able to get my hands on some paperback fiction that the day scholars had passed on to me. I had become friends with a few of them, especially the Nepalese girls, and they supplied me with a steady round of reading material. I read everything I could lay my hands on. Sometimes I would get away with my extra reading, but most of the time, I would get caught. The teacher would embarrass me by making me put whatever I was reading away, but at the next study period, I would be back at it again. I made sure my homework was done, and reading everything I could made up for the lack of newspapers, magazines, radios, or televisions.

There was hardly time for extras in our busy lives. We were constantly supervised, but at 8:30 p.m., we closed our books and were allowed to walk back to our cottages in groups at a leisurely pace. While some had farther to go than others, I always thought myself lucky to be living in Birissa because our cottage was the closest to everything. The boys held their study session in the classroom below us. They started fifteen minutes after us and ended fifteen minutes later so there would be no chance of socializing after dark. The boys' cottages were in the opposite direction of the girls, so no boy had better be caught on the wrong side of the clock tower at the end of the school buildings.

I rather enjoyed these walks back to the cottage, taking in the pitch black of the night. I loved the feeling of being folded in a soft cloak, as I picked out the familiar landmarks standing like comforting sentinels to guide my footsteps home. The skies would be studded with stars, blinking and twinkling in the inky, black sky. I could recognize the Milky Way and the Big and Little Dippers without any trouble. No street lights lit the pathways, and the lights of the little town of Kalimpong were three miles away down in the valley. I knew every stone dip and curve and was sure-footed as I made my way home. The only lights would be the ones in our cottages up on the hills and far away on the next rise. Most of all, I loved the fireflies twinkling during their short season to shine. I never knew until later that you could catch them and put them in jar. We had our electrical torches, but on moonlit nights, how glorious it was to see the jagged line of the pale white, snow-capped mountains. The three tall firs standing silently at the end of Jarvie Hall were always a source of wonder and mystery to me. As I listened to the soft whispering of the wind rustling through the branches, I would imagine clandestine meetings and romances that may have happened among their closely hidden shadows. The faraway Rangeet River in the deep valley, which during the day was a gray wash of meandering water, looked like a silver ribbon in the clear moonlit night, and I knew I would always remember this place of serene beauty for all of my life. There was a night watchman to see us back if we needed him to, but security was never an issue. We were in our own little world and far from any kind of life but our own. I always walked slowly and quietly, reflecting on the day and thinking only of doing it all over again tomorrow.

Once back at the cottage, the seniors would have a little time to themselves. We chatted in the kitchen and discussed all of the events of the day. Soon it would be time to turn out the lights and head upstairs to the dormitory, where we undressed and knelt by our beds for a short prayer.

My prayer every night was the same. I always asked for my parents to come and take me home.

We would be expected to knock on the housemother's door and say goodnight so she would know that everyone was accounted for. As I grew older, I decided to forego the customary nightly peck on the cheek that had been such a big part of my early years and instead uttered a polite goodnight to all before turning in.

Everyone would be in bed by 9:00 p.m. I could hear the clock tower on the school grounds by the great hall sound the hour and the nine bells as I closed my eyes. I fell into exhausted sleep, listening to the sounds of the laughing hyenas that roamed our hills at night and to the wind moaning over and over again as it rushed through the valleys below us. For the longest time, I was scared and nervous of these eerie noises that sounded as if someone was crying all night long, but I soon came to love these nighttime songs, for that is what they were to me. They came to be such a familiar part of my life, along with the mountains, hills and valleys of the place where I grew up. Even to this day, I still feel an affinity with nature, which gives me serenity and pleasure in its beauty.

Our routine would change slightly on the weekends. We slept in an hour later in the mornings, but the housework on Saturday would resemble a very thorough spring-cleaning. Special emphasis was put on leaving no speck of dust behind, and we dug deep to do our best to polish and shine everything. It was usually a more relaxed atmosphere, and as long as we were all done by 10:00 a.m., we could move at our own pace. During the hours that led up to lunch at noon, we could take time for ourselves. The senior girls usually took this time to sit outside in the sun or on the windowsills in the kitchen and locker rooms to try out new hairstyles, go through lockers, or just chat with friends.

After lunch on Saturday, and if all housework was done, we were required to leave our cottage and find something to do. Most of us would usually head to the school playground. No one was allowed to stay in the cottage after 1:00 p.m. The time between then and 3:00 p.m. was reserved for the housemothers and teachers to have the cottage for napping and privacy. Any infractions of this rule were severely dealt with. You could lose privileges, such as cake on Sunday, or you could end up with extra scrubbing duties or even the back of the hairbrush across the back of your legs.

I snuck back many times, sometimes just to see if I could make it without being caught. I was stopped in my attempts more times than I care to remember, until I became proficient at it. Since the cottages were not soundproof, even the slightest footfall could be heard if you were listening for it. I became better and better at it and, even now, can creep around like a cat.

At one particular time, a housemother allowed us to have an old gramophone that we wound up and played size seventy records on. We only had one recording of Bolero, with a slow, uninspiring tune on the other side. We wore out the Bolero side, using its steady beat to dance to. We danced everything to that tune—the foxtrot, the swing, lindy, and even the jitterbug to name a few. We picked up all sorts of odd languages, dance steps, and fashions from the once a month movie we were allowed to watch. Some of the more memorable ones were *The Wizard of Oz, Red Shoes, 20000 Leagues under the Sea, Dick Turpin,* and *Robin Hood.* I later came to know these as some of the best movies ever made. Music was confined to hymns we sang and learning the Indian National Anthem.

Saturday afternoons would find some of the girls going off in groups of twos and threes to wander the hillsides close by looking for wild raspberries and cherries, or fallen walnuts under the huge trees. It was rare to find a good harvest of these items. Since I was always hungry, I would keep my favorite spots a secret. Once in a while we would run across a group of boys chasing butterflies, and I would spot a brother of mine, racing with bare brown legs flashing, his net streaming behind him as he dashed by, trying to capture an elusive beauty on the wing, to add to his collection.

Once a month, we would have a boiled egg for breakfast and a piece of cake with frosting for Sunday tea. On Sundays the usual morning events took place, and after breakfast and singing of hymns, the daily work duties would be lighter than usual. No polishing or scrubbing was needed, just dusting and sweeping up of all floors. Everyone then prepared for Sunday morning church service, which started at ten in the morning. Sunday uniforms included a short-sleeved, button-up blouse, again inspired by your own cottage color, worn under a light blue serge bolero and matching A-line skirt. A white hair ribbon had to be in everyone's hair, and we scrambled to make it to our places in line for the march up to the church by twos. The boys all wore white, long-sleeved cotton shirts and navy blue shorts. Looking down from the edge of the church compound at this time on Sunday morning, a visitor could see all the children in perfect formation by cottages, making their way up the hill, each passing the school clock tower, the three fir trees, and the school classrooms. The procession would slowly round the bend above Calcutta boys' cottage, making its way past the hedges of white mayflowers in full bloom, passing under the cascading red bougainvillea tumbling down the steep overhead bank, and then on to the cobbled pathway of the church with the beautiful rose garden in the center.

The church named for Daddy Graham's wife, Kathryn, was always awe inspiring to me. Built entirely of stone like a small cathedral, it was beautiful and peaceful inside, albeit very cold in winter. Rows upon rows of wooden pews stood on either side of an aisle separating the boys from the girls. In my time, almost a thousand children were living in Dr. Graham's Homes. Add to that the staff of housemothers and teachers, and you would get an idea of this lovely church built to accommodate us all. As each cottage filed in and took their designated places, people quietly looked around to pick out a brother or sister or secret crush, and whispers would be heard throughout. My eyes were always riveted on Hart Cottage, from where my brothers looked back at me with huge eyes and solemn faces as the music teacher played the organ.

My gaze always wandered to the beautiful stained glass windows set in every archway, and the breathtakingly colorful larger ones in the very front of the church, high up toward the ceiling. Smaller ones framed the back arched windows in the gallery, where visitors could attend the services as well. I would later come to know, that most of the glass and furnishings in the church were donations from various people and charities, and the images depicted of the young Jesus as a boy growing up, was so appropriate for Daddy Graham's beloved children.

The service would last about an hour. My favorite part was listening to the choir's soloist, followed by the chorus. A short prayer and benediction followed to end the service, followed by an orderly exit as everyone filed out. I always joined the choir and was especially happy when a kind benefactor donated light blue Indian saris for us to wear to Sunday morning church services, especially as I loved the native dress of my country.

I loved this church. I was at peace in it. I knew that, as soon as the service was over, I would walk out to be greeted by my brothers and bask for a few minutes in their smiles and closeness. At no other time during our school years were we able to come together as we did on Sundays after church service, and for this I give thanks to my oldest brother, who made it an integral part of our little family's life at the beginning of each week. I lived for these moments, clinging desperately to any news of our parents. I could live for the whole week to come on a small scrap of acknowledgement that our parents knew of us and loved us.

The rest of Sunday would go by quickly. We strolled back to our cottages in twos and threes, the formations no longer required, to a lunch of rice and vegetables and a bread or tapioca pudding. We performed more duties, lighter ones, washing and putting away the dishes, and then everyone was expected to be on or in her bed at one o'clock for a two-hour rest. Most of the time, I managed to find a book, but either way, silence was strictly adhered to. At three o'clock, when the two-hour period ended, there was at last time to do whatever it was you liked best until teatime at six. This was story time with the little ones for me, so we found a quiet spot, and I, along with Ching, my cat, would transport the little girls to another world of fantasy and daring, where heroes were beyond brave and heroines grew more and more beautiful.

Sunday tea always brought the treat of cake, which was the duty of the kitchen girls to bake. The gospel hour afterward would ring out with beautiful hymns and choruses being sung by the children. All this would be followed by a couple of hours of letter writing or quiet conversations. I would write to my designated sponsor from UNICEF and draw her pictures, or I would enclose the latest poem I had written. I perfected my handwriting and proudly displayed my letter to the housemother to read, before she sent it to the post office. My sponsor always replied with delight at receiving my correspondence and would enclose a photograph or picture of something I might like. Moments like these were treasured by me, and gratitude fills me even now that someone cared about me.

It was on one Sunday evening such as this that I was encouraged to write a children's story of goblins, wizards, and magic spells, which my favorite housemother put in an envelope to be sent to a publisher in England. After some time, I received a wonderful letter of praise and encouragement from the publisher. Although the subject was not exactly what they were searching for, they loved my story, and I was given much support. I felt elated that I could accomplish something on my own.

One Sunday evening a friend encouraged me to write a letter to a boy who had shown an interest in seeing me. No matter how much I protested, she wouldn't take no for an answer. So I gave in and wrote what she told me to. My friend was a little older than me and very pretty. Things like this came easily to her, but I struggled to get the words on paper as she dictated them to me. I put my foot down when she told me to put x's after my name and to write that I "wish these were real."

After I wrote the letter, the boy asked to see me on a Saturday afternoon away from prying eyes. I think I had already built up a dislike for him at this point, but I had to see it through, ready to do battle if he looked at me with crossed eyes. When I met with him, I sat an arm's length away from him on the grass. Quick as lightning, his arms were around my neck in a death grip, and he was kissing my cheek as I struggled to turn my head away. The only thing I could think of was how I was going to kill my friend, while the boy's hair oil fragrance filled my nostrils and I saw the sweat beading on his forehead. My strength was a good match for him, and when I was free, I knew there would be no more letters sealed with a kiss.

I laugh at this today, especially when I remember waking up the next morning with a stiff neck that stayed with me for a week. I couldn't have been more than eleven years old and still had a long way to go in learning life's lessons.

Reflecting back on all those years, I realize that we girls learned to work hard side by side with each other, to respect each other's efforts, and to accept that this was a natural way of life for everyone. We learned you could have pride in good, honest work, rather than a feeling of being degraded at having to scrub the floors on your hands and knees. I must admit that, when I first left the strict rules of Dr. Graham's Homes and was on my own, I refused to clean anything and wanted no responsibilities. Marriage and a baby brought it all back and I was ever grateful for the knowledge and good sense of that hard work. I am also very grateful for the fact that our food, although somewhat bland, was healthy, therefore giving us a good start in eating the right things, and I don't find it difficult to put aside the tempting morsels that are less healthy.

Chapter 7

During my fourteen years in Dr. Graham's Homes, we all went about barefoot. Daddy Graham himself often went barefoot in these mountains, and whether going without shoes was part of a healthy lifestyle or because of the lack of funds to obtain good footwear, none of us ever gave much thought to our shoeless state. The local Nepalese folk always went about barefoot as well, and apart from stubbed toes and a slash from a rock now and then, they all seemed to have healthy, strong feet. The teachers and housemothers of course, were clad in their own footwear suitable to them. I may have had shoes on twice, and both times I came away with huge blisters on the backs of my heels, so my feet were much better off without them.

In the cold, dry winters, I was plagued with extremely chapped hands, feet, and lips; chilblains in between my toes; and cracks in my heels, but so were some of the other children. When the problems appeared, we were treated at the dispensary and went on about our business of daily life, learning to ignore anything that tried to slow us down.

In the monsoon months, which began in June and ended at the end of August, the children walked to school and continued with after-school activities through sheets of steady downpours every day and night. We all wore rubber capes with hoods, which kept us fairly dry, but no matter what we did, the mildew settled into everything, especially since all the wet clothing had to be air-dried. When the grasses and scrub brush grew thick and tall, our bare feet came in contact with all manner of wet, glossy crawling things. Besides the wet, ankle-deep mud, we also encountered leeches and centipedes.

My first encounter with a leech sticking to the underside of my toe left me paralyzed for several minutes, particularly when I saw the bright red ribbon of blood that was following me. However, my curiosity got the better of me, and soon I learned, along with everyone else, how to grab the bag of rough salt stored in the classroom closet and pour a handful of it onto the hitchhiker clinging to the underside of my toes.

We would always know when the monsoon rain was on its way, because the night before, we had messengers in the form of two-inch, flying, ant-like insects that darkened the skies in the evening, falling to the ground in vast numbers and forming what looked like a tightly woven carpet. I found great difficulty in having to step on them, but my imagination allowed me to think that it was only their wings I was crushing, hoping the actual ant-like insect was burrowing underground before I smashed its little body.

Once, I collected about a half dozen of these flying insects, put them in a box with holes punched into the top, and left them overnight on a shelf in the locker room. The next morning, after opening the cover, I saw nothing but wings in the box, and as I held my breath listening all the while for fearful screams at sight of the escapees, I searched frantically for large ants running around. I couldn't face the possibility of one of them eating the others, but it did cross my mind. I never recovered any of them and still don't know what happened, but at the time, I hoped they had made their escape safely after shedding their wings.

Some of these seasonal occurrences, although making me squeamish to start with, not only stirred my curiosity, but also taught me how to avoid them and, if I was not successful at that, at least how to treat the results of an unpleasant encounter with them. On rare occasions, there was the inevitable attack of hookworms, which were quite worrisome. Some children were more susceptible than others, but the trips to the dispensary to see Sister Cassidy would result in the problem being treated and eventually going away.

Our lack of suitable footwear and our athletic uniforms of white, square-necked, cotton shirts and black, cotton bloomers came under ridicule from some outside schools, against whom we would compete in track-and-field events. While I felt somewhat inferior sometimes, I was confident in our abilities to beat any rival team that came up against us. We soon earned the other teams' respect when, at the end of the day, with our sheer grit and determination, we swept every trophy, and held our heads high as we paraded off the field to thunderous applause. We produced barefoot speedsters left everyone wondering whether shoes were more of a hindrance than an added benefit. We certainly did leave our competitors with a good impression of us. I made friends with many of the girls from other schools, but some just wanted my attention so they could get my brother Mitchell to flash a smile at them. I wished them all good luck in their endeavors.

Girls coming of age were not issued with bras or slips, as these items were usually handed down by some kind soul or, as in my case, made to resemble the real thing from scraps of old cloth, which I would sew together by hand. I remember sitting in a secret place next to my cottage, out of sight of everyone, trying to make a bra that would work for me. I made do until an older girlfriend allowed me to have one of hers, and I was most grateful for this kind gesture. We knew that the finer undergarments were in existence, due to the housemothers having their own delicate lace slips and camisoles. As I grew into my late teens, I was helped by a discerning housemother and teacher, who presented me with some of her own delicate pieces of clothing and a soft slip, which I held most dear, considering myself the luckiest person in the world.

Our uniforms were sewn by a local tailor in Bencraig, a cottage down the hill, and supervised by an experienced home economics housemother. We were measured once a year before the winter set in and fitted with either new or old clothes before the New Year. A casual dress was also issued, which we could wear when school uniforms were not required, such as on Saturday and Sunday afternoons, and this resulted in a nice change for us.

There were occasional parties or social gatherings in the case of older teens, and for these events, there were hand-me-down party frocks available. If you found one that fit you and that you liked this year, it would go to someone else the next year, and the search would begin all over again. I never seemed to have any trouble finding something, and it was always exciting, just knowing there would be a party.

The housemother of a cottage could throw a party for the children if, for instance, the cottage was awarded the swimming or sports shields for the year or for a teachers birthday or even at Christmas. As far back as I can remember, Hart Cottage where my brothers lived always had a party on the day of the gala (or Sports Day), since they were always sure to win the trophies. I was invited to all of them and have some memorable moments of Rick filling a table napkin with all the sweets and savory samosas, which I loved, and allowing me to take the treats back to my friends in the cottage. I also remember my cottage having occasional parties when we performed well on the sports field. At these joyful times, we wore our party frocks and spent happy, carefree hours preparing ourselves for the coming festivities. We laid aside our duties and schoolwork to participate, with smiles and laughter ringing out.

In my last year at Dr. Graham's Homes, I pondered how I would manage to find shoes and clothing for my first year at college. I was the only student in my graduating class who was moving into the educational field, and I realized that my mother would not have the means to outfit me with much in the way of linens and clothing. I decided to visit the housemother in Bencraig, where all our clothes were made and stored, and asked for her help. She was very kind to me, offering to supply me with linens an athletic outfit to wear that was entirely different from the black bloomers, and a trunk to carry everything in.

I considered myself very fortunate to have this lifeline thrown to me, when along came a young teacher who was leaving to go abroad. She mentioned her plight, similar to mine several years earlier, and I will never forget the kind gesture on her part. The clothes she passed on to me were lovely and required no alterations. I got everything I needed and more, including a gorgeous party frock in my favorite color at the time. I realized I had been very apprehensive about everything coming to an end for me and was wondering if I had the confidence to go out on my own. This single gesture, this act of kindness offered to me enabled me to gain the confidence I needed so desperately. Prayers again were being answered.

Chapter 8

I hadn't seen either of my parents in years. My longing and yearning to see them was never felt more than at the end of the school year, when classes and school activities were suspended from the first week in December to the first week in March.

Beginning in early November "the list" was posted on the bulletin board at the post office. To me, this was the most important document of the year, at least until I turned seventeen. Every year, parents would send train and bus ticket fares for their children's trip home for the Christmas holidays. As the money was received, the children's names would appear on the list. During this time and after school was over for the day, children raced down the pathways, rushing past the hedgerows and skipping over stone steps, all headed in the same direction—to read the names on the list at the post office. Each person or family listed would be going home to his or her parents. I was always there as well, hoping that by a miracle this would be the year that my name would appear on the list.

That was not to be. The Hayes name never appeared, at least not for going home with our parents. In all those years of hoping and wanting and racing down the hill, the disappointments became easier to bear as the years went by.

My name did appear once when I was fourteen, but it was not because of my parents. Most children had their own homes to go to and only about twenty-five to thirty children were left behind. Efforts were made by the staff throughout the year, and throughout India, for a temporary home for the rest of us without a place to go—a place where we could enjoy

Christmas away from the school, in a loving environment. These were foster homes, so to speak, for three months at Christmas. I was not chosen until I was fourteen. A middle-aged Swedish couple wanted two teenage girls, and I was chosen.

This was a wonderful and eye-opening experience in many ways, given the sheltering we received at Dr. Graham's Homes. On this holiday, I learned how to use a telephone; how to shoot a .22 rifle, for which I won a trophy; and how to take better care of my skin, wear pretty clothes, and eat wonderful food. I was miles away from Dr. Graham's Homes, and I ran into an old acquaintance of my father's, met some new people who were quite nice to me, heard Elvis Presley sing for the first time, and fell into a trance every time I heard Pat Boone's "Love Letters in the Sand."

We spent the last week before the holidays wrapping things up at school. We held the last social dance and attended the end-of-the-school year award ceremonies, speeches, and school plays, and all the classrooms were locked up until the next year. Yes, it was an exciting time. The downside was saying good-bye to friends who would be gone for two to three months. Some would come back; others would not. Then there were the new children, who would start to trickle in toward the end of February.

All the children who went home packed their little suitcases and started wearing their shoes again to break them in. December was the most exciting month of the year, as some parents would send new clothes to travel in, knowing that their children would have outgrown the clothes they'd had a year ago upon arriving for the start of the previous school year. The rest of us who were not going home were also caught up in all the excitement.

In the early years, I would pack a little box for myself, thinking that I may get to go home as well. The excitement was contagious, and eventually "going home day" arrived. It always came around my birthday on December 5. The weather was starting to get considerably colder, but we still had some bright, sunny days left. Discipline was a little less rigid on this day, and children were allowed to walk around saying their good-byes and catching up with friends, visiting from one cottage to another, promising to write and to bring back goodies when they returned. Several Jeeps, Land Rovers, and other four-wheel-drive vehicles were hired from the town of Kalimpong, seven miles below us. They made the steep trip up to Dr. Graham's Homes, where they waited in single file in front of the post office.

The children would be transported down the mountain to the buses waiting in the market square. Only very rugged and sturdy vehicles with their very experienced Nepali drivers could make the tough trip, and we watched from our lofty cottages and rocky perches as the Jeeps would slowly wind their way up and around one hairpin turn after another. Some of the turns and bends required three-point turns because they were so sharp and steep. The whining of the motors could be heard as the gears were shifted to accommodate the next turn. Every time there was a break in the lush treetops and thick foliage, we could see the slow-moving vehicles as they made their way up to our post office. Once they arrived and lined up one behind the other, the children going home would be seen making their way toward them from their cottages, carrying their suitcases, some running ahead and some waiting for their friends or family to catch up.

Organized chaos was the order of the day. About five hundred to six hundred children had to board an assortment of vehicles, making sure families were together and everyone was accounted for. Soon the last stragglers were on the last Jeep, and the side doors were locked tight. How many slender teenagers and tiny children could you pack in one of those Jeeps? There were no limits or passenger seating rules, and no seat belts to be checked and secured.

You could see happy smiles and arms and legs flailing inside, but everyone knew to hang on tight and keep all arms tucked inside. Even though, at first, children were hanging out of the windows and yelling and calling out to each other, the first Jeep did not move until all was secure and the staff had checked everyone on their lists.

The rest of us staying behind would dash down the stone pathways, taking a shortcut to the first bend in the road, to wave frantically as the convoy of vehicles rolled by. My throat would be hoarse afterward from all the cheering I had done to give my classmates a good send-off. The smell of petrol and diesel lingered in my nostrils for the rest of the day, and I found it to be not so unpleasant.

In my midteens, those of us who wanted to could ride down to the market with our friends who were leaving. But once they were loaded onto the buses for the sixty-mile trip to the Siliguri train station, we would have to trek back up the mountain on our own, a trip that was five miles of rough footpaths cut out of the rocky hillside, and all the time, we would be steadily climbing. The views were spectacular along the way, and if we took our time, we could make it back to our cottage in about two hours. The boys of course, raced back and could do the trip in less time.

The children would board the buses in the market square, and I pictured the bus ride in my mind, knowing they would be winding their way farther and farther down the mountainside, leaving the hills of the school behind. In my mind, this route, which I was to take many times before I left India, was the most beautiful I had ever seen. The forests were lush with firs and evergreens, waterfalls, and wild rare orchids high up in the treetops. At occasional rest stops, the Langur monkeys came out of hiding and sat nearby, looking for a morsel or two, and the villagers in their tiny shops moved about with a carefree spirit and ready smile as the Nepali people always do. There was just one single-lane, paved road, so the bus driver would honk his horn as he approached a bend, and there were hundreds of bends. As a matter of fact, I was always one of the unlucky few who became quite ill at the start of the trip, but like everything else, you dealt with it and overcame it as best you could.

I remember once, when the driver saw my distress, he stopped to cut a few sprigs off a nondescript bush, which he crushed in the palm of his hand and which he held out for me to inhale. I immediately found my nausea was relieved.

If a rare vehicle was approaching from the opposite direction, it seemed the proper etiquette was to let the climbing vehicle go by first. The Jeep or bus going down would be pressed against the rising wall of cliff and forest, while the passing vehicle would seem suspended over a sheer drop with the ravine far below. I remember holding my breath for fear I would be the one to tip the passing bus over, to plunge all the way down to the rocks below. As a matter of fact, I remember all banter and laughter coming to an abrupt end until the incident was over with. The Nepali drivers found a cheerful way to deal with it and each other, and as we all released our collective breath, the driver would continue with his melodious folk song, and we would soon all be at ease again. The drivers were expert at the wheel, and the jostling about was done in great humor and laughter. No bus or child was ever in jeopardy.

I pictured the buses creeping their way across the Teesta River over a solid concrete and steel bridge that the British helped build during the time of their occupation of India. The bridge was and is still used as a checkpoint for all nonlocals or foreign tourists and hikers. It was the only connection across the river and was heavily guarded by the military. All traffic from the surrounding hills of Darjeeling, Kalimpong, Kurseong and surrounding hill stations converged at the Teesta Bridge, and all were stopped and cleared before they could go on. During the Tibetan and Chinese conflict, the flow of traffic back and forth was heavy and everyone was either allowed access or not, according to whom they were.

Once everyone arrived in Siliguri, the chaperones, usually teaching staff, would make sure all the children were on the right trains to take them home to their parents. Most of them would go south to Calcutta, while the rest would catch trains to places like Gauhati, Assam, and Shillong, taking them further west and to the north. The trip would last a couple of days by train. Those going to Calcutta would have to cross the Brahmaputra River by ferry and continue on the train until they pulled into Sealdah station in Calcutta, where most of their parents would be waiting.

I would follow them on their long trips in my mind. I would be lost in the stillness and silence that followed the departure of the last Land Rover. I felt suspended in a lonely place devoid of all emotions.

The feeling did not last long, and I was soon looking around for my brothers so we could talk about the events of the day. We were not bitter or angry, but a familiar sadness hovered over us for a while.

I will always remember that little post office. I can still smell the somewhat musty odors of the letters, files, and heavy leather mailbags, which I associate so vividly with my childhood.

As I wound my way back to the only cottage still left open for the few children left behind, my mind was already leaping ahead of my footsteps, and I was looking forward to the slight easing up of the rigid restrictions, which would be slackened briefly for a short time. I thought about the girls I would be living with for the next three months and all the names were familiar. It seemed to be the same families every year that stayed behind, and none of us were particularly interested in what the other one was doing. But I learned to make the best of any situation at a very early stage in my life, and knew I would be all right with everything, once this loneliest of all days was over.

I still had my brothers, who I could see more often now, so long as they were not on some butterfly hunting trip or roaming the hillsides for things to eat. After all, they were luckier, in that the boys could go off in groups by themselves, free to roam and explore, and my brothers almost always stayed together. I didn't have a sister at the time, so I was lonelier than most.

I still envied the ones with homes to go to. After all, they wouldn't have to scrub floors and toilets and wash dishes every day. They would get to eat curry and rice and home-cooked food like *gelabies* and *goolab jamuns* whenever they wanted to. I would have to eat the plain food every day, except for Christmas, when we would likely get to make a Christmas pudding.

I could look forward to that. In the meantime, I would fall back on the things I enjoyed doing, like coloring, drawing, reading already read books, knitting, and talking and playing with my imaginary friends, who were mostly tiny faeries, and I lived with them under toadstools. I also sewed a lot of clothes by hand for my rag doll. I built my own little lean-to shelter out of sticks and stones behind the washhouse, where I could sit by myself and dream my dreams and imagine myself as Dick Turpin, the highway robber who was always rescuing the damsel in distress. For some reason I was always rescuing someone and I can't remember dreaming princess dreams.

I was happiest at these times. My brother Mitchell would visit on Saturdays, and sometimes he would sit in my little shack. I would just enjoy him being there. We never talked of our father and mother; we didn't have anything to go on. In fact, we didn't talk much at all. We would sit and look out over the surrounding hillsides to the Himalayas and the silvery ribbon of water winding its way so far away down in the valley. At this time of year, the hillsides would be brown and bare and bleak, with no signs of the sparkling lushness so prevalent during the summer and after the monsoon rains. The weather would turn so much colder. The days would be short, and the nights would be crisp and darker than dark.

The Himalayas were constant and never lost their beauty at any time of the year. I could always look to the Himalayas, silent, constant, and majestic. They never left me to go home for the Christmas holiday. When I first opened my eyes to the misty morning, I could look at their jagged outline through my dormitory window with its billowy curtains. With just a hint of the lightening sky, I would know that the mountains were always there. I would watch as first the shapes and then the play of light and colors would sweep across the range, from gray to purple to red, orange, and yellow, and finally the sparkling sun reflected off them. During my very early years, I always knew they were there, and I used them as a beacon to show me the way and guide my barefoot steps home. As I grew older, and withdrew from most, I looked to the Himalayas as my constant, beautiful friend, at peace with me in my silence, crying with me in my anger and frustration of growing up and wondering where my parents were. On this very lonely night in the beginning of winter, I fell asleep and allowed myself to be enfolded and cradled by them and to dream my dreams of a home of my own.

Chapter 9

As the years floated slowly by, I learned the routines and was able to abide by the rigid rules. I learned to pray five or six times a week, to sing hymns, and lead a Christian life. I learned not to look for my mother or father at every turn, but I knew, through my oldest brother Ivan, that they were somewhere out there in the vast world. I still waited for the day they would come back and take me away with them. This one thought sustained me through most of my life in Dr. Graham's Homes, and I never doubted, not even once, that it would not come true. I learned that some children didn't have any parents at all. They never received cards or letters like I sometimes did from my mother. Some children went home for the Christmas Holidays, and some, like me did not. The ones who did have a home to go to were considered to be the luckiest of all. They were missed terribly when they were gone and envied when they returned, as they told us wonderful stories of freedom and happiness with loving parents. I learned and I accepted, and as my chest tightened, I kept my empty heart closed to all feelings except ones of sadness and loneliness.

Not all of the days were dark and bleak. There were also fun times and happy excursions, like the days we went on picnics in the hills. We packed sandwiches and cake and drank our tea by the open fire, where we sang our favorite songs. We were free to roam the rarely used paths looking for treasure or hidden surprises. I experienced joy in my surroundings and used my imagination, pretending to be a great explorer or Captain Nemo from *20,000 Leagues*. My great love for the outdoors was nurtured at a very young age, and I quickly came to realize that being alone sometimes was where I most wanted to be.

Somehow, I succeeded in this much too often, resulting in some kind of punishment. The constant chattering of too many voices was enough to send me searching for a quieter place. Even now, a few hours of solace every day allows me time for reflection and the luxury to breathe in fresh air.

Making friends was not easy for me. The harder I tried to build a bridge, the further away I got from my goal. I seemed to lack the right combination of self-confidence and sincerity toward my fellow residents. The one or two friendships I was able to form have remained with me throughout my life. I had been given a large helping of empathy for people in need. My young friend who was stricken with polio became my constant companion for several years. I imposed my own rules on myself, and the walls around my heart hardened. I kept almost everyone at bay, my peers, the teachers, the housemothers, and every other adult who crossed my path. I only know that inside the hard walls, my heart yearned for tenderness and to nurture or be nurtured.

The housemothers gave up on making a sweet, compliant child out of me. I obeyed when I had to and rebelled when I could, and I took punishment from my superiors stoically and without emotion.

Then one day, we were introduced to a new housemother. This new person planted herself right in the middle of my chaotic, turbulent, closed little life and succeeded in almost toppling the walls built up around me. She stayed for five years, and very soon after she took up residence in Birissa Cottage, I found myself wanting to give into her nurturing and caring ways. There was sincerity in the way she loved the children she was in charge of, and for the first time since my mother left, I felt warmth creeping into my body for an adult. Up until now, I had classified all of them as not to be trusted with any of my emotions. Her name was Miss Ellen Dailey, and she, more than anyone, epitomized the true meaning of what Dr. Graham tried to accomplish during his lifetime. She was a missionary who was dedicated to the abandoned children of Dr. Graham's Homes, and the inhabitants of Birissa Cottage, and especially me, were the most fortunate of all the children to have had this bright light thrust into our young lives.

I turned eleven and had learned to like going to school more and more.

It was so much better than living life in Birissa Cottage, where the routines were harsh and offered no rewards. I yearned for sporting and cultural events—competitions of any kind and physical exercise—where I could lose myself, and gain the recognition and popularity that these things brought. I was a different person on the playing field and often laughed and cheered at all our accomplishments and antics.

It was during this time that Miss Ellen Dailey, from Australia, arrived on the scene, to take over as housemother in my cottage. We would address her as Aunty Ellen, which was very different because we always addressed the housemothers by their last names. As usual, I had nothing to say to her. I would clam up when asked a simple question and let her know in an instant that I had no use for another strange adult in my life. I more or less sneered at all the usual favorites, gushing and simpering around our new aunty. In the back of my mind, I silently wished I could let her put her arm around me, but I also knew that I would never allow it to happen. I was going to let her know, in my own way, that I was in control of who did or didn't get inside my feelings.

Very efficiently, very calmly, the cottage seemed to take on a subtle change under Aunty Ellen's "housemothering." I noticed that, after a short time, I would walk around without looking downcast, and my name was not being called out every few minutes because I'd failed to do something I should have. I found myself not wanting to fight all the time and became softer toward most people. I learned to tolerate my enemies and eventually yearned for a smile and a hug from a grown-up who was silently working her way into my heart. I learned that she was not the enemy but, rather, someone who sought me out and took the time to talk with me. She was someone who knew, somehow, that she was not allowed to speak of my beloved parents without my permission, to me or anyone else. She knew the sacredness of this subject tied with a secret ribbon and wrapped inside my heart. Little did I know, she would get even closer to unraveling my secrets.

Aunty Ellen was young, about twenty-five, and had short, blond hair that came just below her ears with fringe (bangs) across her forehead. She had twinkling, blue eyes and a ready smile, and although she was not plump, she was of medium height and had an attractive look about her. She had a happy, sunny disposition that was infectious and was a complete change from the other housemothers we'd previously come to know.

We would later find out that Aunty Ellen was engaged to be married to someone overseas. This was exciting and mysterious to the young teenage girls, who dreamed of handsome princes and faraway places.

I remember walking into a very serious discussion of where babies came from, with Aunty Ellen sitting on a bench surrounded by wide-eyed, awestruck preteens and older girls as they asked questions and were given gentle, uncomplicated answers. I never intended to stick around, but I looked forward to the lesson on baking scones I thought was taking place but would actually come a few minutes later. My fair hair and skin always stood out among the others, which made me hard to miss in a small gathering, and so it was that twinkling, blue eyes met wary blue-green ones, and I felt myself being compelled to stay for the rest of the discussion. I learned at that time the proper names for parts of the body, and we talked openly but hesitatingly about what most of the girls only whispered about, which had been a subject unfit for discussion by anyone.

Being one of the few children left behind for the Christmas holidays, I was faced with the prospect of not seeing the few friends I had for almost three months. I was forced to make new ones from some of the other cottages. I was twelve and somehow got the feeling that this holiday would be different, even though I was not yet able to look beyond my feelings of loneliness, insecurity, and emptiness. I would spend my spare time wandering the now quiet school grounds and nearby hillsides, in search of wild berries or unusual wildflowers. My steps sometimes took me far out of shouting distance.

I spent the evenings with Aunty Ellen listening to stories of the evangelist Billy Graham, singing along with the gospel songs that were played on the gramophone, or getting lost in the glorious sounds of the Mormon Tabernacle Choir. The winter nights were cold, the days dismal and bleak with a sudden day of sunshine here and there.

Since there were no suitable warm clothes, Aunty Ellen miraculously produced dozens of knitting needles and skeins of red wool and I proceeded to knit my first cardigan. The initial result was a cardigan with dropped stitches and one sleeve longer than the other. I learned fast though and soon produced near perfect results, helping others along the way. I can still remember the first Sunday when all the girls from Birissa Cottage showed up in church proudly wearing their red cardigans. The rest of the cottages soon followed, suit producing their own color-coordinated outerwear.

It was around this time that I felt the first "crack" in the walls around my heart. What Aunty Ellen did was not very perceptible. Her approach was rather subtle. She would seek me out specifically for advice or input on day-to-day occurrences. For some time, I had been playing with ways to coax little crawling bugs out of their shells. I even had imaginary friends, like a dog or a cat, as we weren't allowed to keep any pets. Seeing my affinity for all things outdoors, Aunty Ellen had taken me under her wing, teaching me how to grow the best roses and care for them under her guidance. She liked the way I had of talking to the roses she taught me to grow. She showed me how to take the spent tea leaves from the teapot and scatter them around the base of the rosebushes, giving them the much-needed acidity they craved. I still treat my roses this way and am never disappointed in their performance. She spoke to my heart, for these were things I loved, and I was going to swallow the bait and be forever in her power if I was not careful. I held back some more, giving her a small notch of approval, and waited to see if this was real.

She continued to involve me in projects and ideas, especially for the smaller children. I started the Sunday afternoon story time, with me as the storyteller. I loved telling stories and put my wild imagination to work, leading the little ones on journeys of bravery, romance, and hair-raising escapades. She encouraged me to read the newspapers that came to her in the mail, and for the first time, I realized that, beyond my small, little world, there were kids like me leading very different lives. They lived in grand houses and wore their own clothes, bought in glamorous shops. I studied the latest fashions, fostering my love of scarves, hats, and blended colors, which I still love today. I showed great interest in solving the crossword puzzle that was always on page three of the paper, and Aunty Ellen was only too pleased to help. I read voraciously, and Saturday afternoons would find me sitting with the outdated newspaper in my lap.

Between my love for sports, reading, storytelling, and household duties, I had little time to wonder about my parents return. Or maybe I was slowly realizing that I was not going to see them any time soon. I caught a glimpse of how pleasant life could be and a promise from Ellen that I would experience this other world on my own. Listening to her, I felt that it could happen.

The Christmas season was soon upon us. One Sunday evening after the usual gospel sing-along, Aunty Ellen announced that we were all going to write down the one thing we would like for Christmas. We all looked at each other with our mouths open, not believing what we had just heard. I remember being puzzled, because the usual Christmas presents came in the form of donated dolls, coloring books, and odd items gathered from various charities. We were used to waking up on Christmas morning to find a white pillowcase hanging from the foot of our beds, in which we found something we could not live without. A handful of sweets tied up in a white paper table napkin and an orange were included as well, much to our delight.

I could see people writing already, but I was undecided, going from one subject to another in my mind. Throughout my stay in Dr. Graham's Homes so far, no one had ever been allowed to keep a pet of any kind, so I kept a bug or two, my favorite being a turquoise beetle that had a shimmering shell around it. I would capture one and keep it in a box with holes on the top, and in a day or two, I would release it back outdoors. Dogs were never seen or heard from, and they lived only in my imagination. Above all else, I wanted a kitten. I also wanted perfume; a lovely, pink party dress; and hair ribbons, as did most of the other girls who were writing down their choices. Each of us was asked to pick three items and write them down, with the most important one being first and so on. My first choice was the kitten, and my own bottle of perfume was second. I had no third choice. We wrote our names on top and folded our lists and handed them in to Aunty.

Three weeks later, with none of us daring to hope that our wishes would come to fruition a large package arrived and was hurriedly whisked away to a secret place in Aunty Ellen's room. I was pensive, knowing there was no kitten in that box, but also knowing that my first wish was impossible to grant. Again I had reluctantly let Aunty Ellen know the contents of my heart, and I vowed to myself that I would fight against showing her any emotion when the day came and the certainty of the absent kitten was revealed. I was glad that no one knew of anyone else's wish list, so I was safe from any side looks and secret mocking smiles from the others.

The parcel, which we now knew contained our precious gifts, was brought to the kitchen table later on Christmas Eve. I could not believe that I was about to be given something of my very own, something not touched by any other hands, which had not been owned by someone else before.

One by one, the little containers were lifted out and carefully wrapped in colorful paper and ribbons. The older girls helped with the packaging, and each of us had to leave the room when it was our gift that was to be wrapped. The excitement and anticipation was beyond anything I had ever experienced, and having to wait until the next morning, when all would be revealed at the Christmas breakfast table, was almost unbearable.

Christmas morning arrived, and although I had given up the idea of the kitten a long time ago, I was excited as I opened the little box with my name on it, curiously happy at having something that was for me and me only. I received a small yellow box, and upon opening it, I found a tiny bottle of what I knew was the perfume I had asked for. She had chosen cherry blossom for me, and I felt the "crack" as my heart and mind absorbed this kind gesture shown to all of us. She even knew how much I loved the cherry blossom trees that covered the hillsides in early spring, dressing up our valleys and tree-shaded pathways in pink and white lace.

It was a moment before I raised my eyes to see her looking at me with a sweet smile. I smiled back and never mentioned the kitten then or after. Along with the perfume, she gave each of us a gift of a pretty, embroidered handkerchief, and we used these gifts, on Sunday mornings, hidden safely in the pockets of our skirts. I never felt as special as I did then.

Life went on sublimely, and about three months after Christmas, I came home from school one afternoon with my friend Louise wrapped across my back. After depositing her in front of her locker, I was given a summons to the staff sitting room. I quickly processed any number of reasons for the messenger's foreboding message.

At a loss to come up with anything substantial, I made my way down the hall, ready to defend myself. I stepped into the staff tearoom, and my spine stiffened as I thought to myself that this was where Aunty Ellen would fall apart. This was when she would reveal her true self, and I would be proved right about her all along.

I barely glanced at a box on the table but noticed that the junior aunty was also in the room, and I was ready to do battle if that proved necessary. Aunty Ellen reached into the box and withdrew a sleepy, little, furry body, which she handed to me. I gazed down at the sweetest little black face and looked into two bright blue eyes, blinking sleepily at me. I held a Siamese kitten in my hands, and as I slowly lifted its body closer to my heart, I found both aunties smiling at my pure joy and delight. My heart somersaulted, and tears, which had had no place in my life before, gathered in my eyes.

I named her Ching. I could never fully express how much this tiny, living creature meant to me. In retrospect and thinking back on those five years with Ellen Dailey, I believe she knew she was not breaking into my tightly held emotions and that I was still lost in my own world. The fact that she picked just the right time and the right gesture to get me to reach out to her made me admit that she, more than anyone, made a lasting impact on my life and, in a way, saved me from giving into anger and destroying everything I held dear. The crack in my heart widened, and I felt a floating sensation, a letting go of the wall I had clung to, and I was not afraid to plant my feet firmly on the ground. She trusted me with the precious life of Ching. I would be solely responsible for the kitten's wants and needs, a task I took up with the greatest of joy. Nothing so far in my past life—not all the awards, not any of the treasured keepsakes I had accumulated—could compare with this.

Ching was soon followed by Chang, a male Siamese, and for about a year, I spent all my devotion on these two, with Aunty Ellen looking on approvingly. She saw my need to nurture and with her watching I improved daily, finding happiness in my existence and looking forward to the next day and new antics of the kittens. I joined everyone else in doing more and helping out with extra tasks, giving my life to God and being saved at a Life for Youth Rally. I liked being around Aunty Ellen and sought her presence when I could.

Sadly, Chang developed distemper after a short while, and there was no way to save him. Aunty Ellen allowed me to carry him to the hospital a couple of miles away to see if the sister in charge could help. After an injection, I carried Chang all the way back, only to have him die that night. I remember Louise, my other friend Joan, and myself putting him in a box wrapped in an old towel and placing him in a hole in the ground. The three of us stood around wondering what to do, when Louise broke into a popular hymn we used to sing. We sang "Low in the Grave He lay," and oddly enough, I felt a giggle escape me at the choice of the hymn.

We said good-bye to my beloved friend, and I missed Chang's warm, little body terribly, but I still had Ching, and she would live on with me by her side every step of the way. No one ever saw me without her wrapped around my shoulders or walked by my bed at night without noticing the telltale lump under my blanket. I fed her whatever I had, along with a little milk I was able to scrape up for her. Mostly she hunted outside for rats and little furry things to eat. She was still alive and well when I left, but I heard that, very soon after I had left for college, she simply went away and never came back.

Waking the aunty at five in the morning was the responsibility of one of the older girls. It would be her duty to creep down the stairs to the kitchen, rake out the ashes from the still warm fire grate, fill the top with fresh coal, and wait for the teakettle to boil. During the cold winter months, when the weather was windy and freezing, the task of going out in the black predawn hours to the coal go-down was one of the toughest things we had to do. Once we were back inside though, it wouldn't be long before the stove would be warm as toast.

I liked this time in the morning, in the silence, with Ching meowing softly as she pranced in and out of my feet. Once the kettle had steam pouring out of its spout, a fresh pot of tea would soon be on its way upstairs to the senior aunty. I learned very early that warming the teapot for a minute with hot water was the key to making the best pot of tea, and the red-gold, steaming liquid poured into a cup first thing in the morning was the only way to start the day. It had to be just right, and Aunty Ellen, toward the end of her stay with us, found me making the tea to her liking. It had to be me every morning, and she would insist that I put a mug on the tray for myself when I brought the tea in to wake her. I wouldn't stay to drink with her but, rather, hurried back downstairs to get a start on my daily duties, nursing my cup and seeking the warmth of the cozy kitchen.

While the children performed the daily work duties in the cottage, the aunties would be busy measuring out stores for the day, as they moved from the storeroom to the larder, where milk, butter, eggs, and vegetables were stored. We had no refrigeration, so the larder was the cold room, made completely with stone or slate slabs for shelving and a small, wire mesh window that opened to the outside, allowing for cool air to pass through it.

The children kept the cottages in order, and the only outside person allowed in was the cook or *borchee* as we called him. He usually lived with his family in the surrounding hills close by and walked to and from the cottage to prepare breakfast, lunch, and dinner meals, making several trips a day. Each cottage had a different cook, and sometimes he would bring his family in on party days to join in the fun.

Later, and after I had been gone from Dr. Graham's Homes for several years, food preparation in the cottages was done away with, and a central feeding program was installed. The children all sat down together in the great hall for their meals. I think this saved the school a lot of money and made for less cleaning up in the cottages.

In my time, the cook ruled the kitchen. If you were on his good side, though, you might be lucky enough to get to lick the custard pot when he was done preparing it for the aunty. During Ellen's stay with us, I learned how to turn out a fluffy omelet in a double boiler and make smooth, delicious custard, among other tasty dishes that made their way to the staff table. Scones were almost a staple for the staff, and I learned the baking process so well it landed me an award at the annual flower show several years in a row. One of the more unappetizing dishes served to the children was a huge, scooped-out cucumber, about eight inches in diameter and over a foot long, filled with ground meat, or mince as we called it. Then the whole thing was baked in the oven, sliced, and served warm. An onion or black pepper may have helped, but these were scarce, and I dreaded those huge cucumbers when they were in season.

For the most part, my brothers and I stayed healthy, until I fell critically ill in my ninth year. Hunger was always present in my childhood. As a result, I would often go looking for something I could eat to stop some of the hunger pains. I discovered the wild cherries that grew profusely on our steep slopes, and on one particular afternoon, I either ate too many of them or ate something along with them that caused me to be sick.

I was found the next morning lying on the floor next to my bed, inert and unresponsive. A hand-carried note, or chit, was hastily sent to the headmaster. Four senior boys rushed from their class to Birissa Cottage, carrying a stretcher on their shoulders. After the boys carried my inert body to the stretcher, I was rushed to the hospital. I was then driven by Jeep to the Chateris Hospital, seven miles away in the town of Kalimpong. I was diagnosed with peritonitis, and although the events were very vague, I remember opening my eyes finally and finding myself in a stark, white room with a nurse in a white uniform sitting in a chair beside my bed. She offered me a sweet, which she said was glucose and this candy, was all I could have to eat for several weeks.

I don't remember exactly how long all of this took, but it had been weeks of special care. I eventually graduated from the glucose to calf's foot jelly, and if I thought the long forgotten bread balls were hard to swallow, this unappetizing, opaque, gray gooey stuff was enough to turn my stomach just by looking at it. This alone was my diet for about three months.

At the end of six months, I was skin and bones and weak as a baby. I had to learn how to walk again and was carried into the sunshine for an hour every morning. No visitors had been allowed at first, but Ivan came by one day bringing a coloring book and some crayons that his teachers had given him for me.

Even after I was allowed back to school just for half-day sessions, I had already lost most of the year and had to repeat the class again. I was mortified but made good headway once I was fully recovered.

When I mentioned my year of this life-threatening illness to my mother, her response was vague, and she seemed to know very little about it. It seemed that my parents could not be contacted at the time, but the word was carried as far as Calcutta that a child from Dr. Graham's Homes, was at death's door in the Charteris Hospital. All efforts were being made to save her life, and only prayer would help. On the night of the crisis, the Presbyterian Church in Calcutta was filled to capacity, as an all-night vigil was kept. My mother remembered going to the vigil, but had no idea that it was me everyone was praying for.

I never brought up the subject again with her, as I thought I detected a look of bewilderment in her eyes. I knew that, during this time of my struggle to stay alive, my mother and father separated, and he went away never to return.

I was given the best care by all the doctors and nurses at the time, and I could never repay my debt to them all. Because of the power of prayer and the expert care from everyone concerned, I am here to tell my story.

I was very fortunate that all this happened under Aunty Ellen's watch. Later, with the arrival of Ching, I was able to turn my thoughts to being less tough on people and life in general. I came out of my shell to embrace happiness and allowed myself to experience joy. I was learning to be around adults without expecting to be disliked by them, to trust when I previously wouldn't or couldn't, and to accept good things that happened my way. I know that, if I had not had this person in my young life, I could have turned out very different and not for the better. I feel as though she pulled me back from a steep precipice, which I was very close to falling down, one that would have been hard to climb back out of. I was despairing of ever finding my parents, and all love was gone from me. I did things in a matter-of-fact sort of way. I ran harder than anyone, I swam faster, and tried more daring things than anyone else. Everything just went by me, to be forgotten and left in my wake. I transformed under this housemother, who gave me a certain amount of love and good attention, and I am forever grateful for the five years under her care. I only regret that I was never able to thank her personally. But the memory of her kindness is stamped on my heart forever.

Sadly, Aunty Ellen's tour of duty at Dr. Graham's Homes ended, and she returned to her fiancé. At fifteen years of age, I found that the impending departure of a loving adult in my life caused my emotions to surface. Once again, I felt a sense of loss at knowing I would be left behind. I was older now and could accept the inevitable circumstances of being on my own. I would go on as I had before she had come.

Toward Aunty Ellen's final departure date, I did not seek her out but stayed with Ching close by my side all day and night. Was I trying to punish her for leaving? Did she know how much I needed her to stay?

On the final day as we all stood in a line to give her a rounding send off, I stood at the end of the line with Ching in her usual place around my neck, not able to say a word to Ellen. She wrapped her sun-freckled arms around me and spoke in my ear, for no one else heard her words. She spoke of how much she regretted that she would not be there for the next few years, when I would become captain of the school and be the leader she envisioned me to be.

Her words became very prophetic, and in a couple of years, I would be nominated for vice captain and lead the girls' athletic teams to many a victory, finding my own identity both on and off the playing fields.

Ellen stood out as the most important adult in my early youth, and I am ever grateful to have been so very lucky that our paths crossed. God had looked down upon me and lent a helping hand!

Chapter 10

Apart from India's Independence Day, the most important holiday of the year was the birthday of The Homes on September 24. This day usually began with a beautiful church service, in which our beloved founder was honored and praised for his faith in God and his love of children. Award ceremonies for swimming events usually followed in the early afternoon, which took place in the main hall at school. Speeches were made by the senior students. Then former boys and girls related some of their past encounters with Daddy Graham. After this, the children and staff made their way to the larger playing field. Each cottage gathered together to form a circle on the ground, and everyone received fresh hot cross buns filled with plump raisins and sweetened fruit, along with a golden, sticky, sweet Indian confection known as a *jelabee*. Along with all of this, we drank cups of steaming hot tea, served up in billycans, making this, by far, the best meal of the year. In the evening, there would either be a good picture show to watch, or the staff would perform hilarious skits and pantomimes. This holiday, for many reasons, was the most memorable to me, and I learned of a gentle man who gave safe shelter and a home to so many children in need.

By far the best prolonged holiday was the two weeks in the very beginning of the year, when we left the cold winter days behind us to bask in a sunshine valley, whose beauty takes my breath away even now. There was something akin to excitement in the air, when the day of departure arrived. Even though we were on the leeward side of the Himalayas, the cold month of January brought harsh, dry winds blowing down from the mountains, across the valleys, and up to the hills where we lived. While the winters rarely ever brought snow to our hill station, we would nevertheless experience bitter cold days and the bleakness of parched, wind-dried trees and forests. Days were short, and nights seemed to never end. To add to this forlorn scenery was the loneliness of being left at the school for the long Christmas holidays, without your friends and with very little going on, to pass the hours. To break up the monotony, the sixteen or so children who were left in the cottage would be treated to a two-week holiday in the warm Teesta Valley, which was about seven miles away.

The Teesta River was one of northern India's most famous rivers. Not only did it bring life to local inhabitants, it also produced spectacular waterfalls and scenic, lush forests and was a tourist attraction for the avid, white water rafters and adrenalin-seeking kayakers. During winter, when the free-flowing waters were tightly encased and trapped in the glaciers of the Himalayan Mountains, the river became calmer but was still fast flowing, giving rise to gentler and more peaceful streams and waterways that broke away from the main body, to form lovely pools and babbling brooks along the way.

One of these small tributaries formed the Rilli Valley where the few inhabitants, mostly Nepalese, farmed sweet potatoes and banana and coconut trees. They also terraced the gentler slopes to plant their rice crops, which when harvested, would be carried in baskets on their backs and transported on foot to the main Teesta Stop by the Coronation Bridge. This bridge, built by the British and heavily patrolled by the military, boasted a thriving little community. It was an important crossroads, from which people traveled to and from the main kingdoms and small independent principalities bordering the northern boundary of India. The small population of people living in the Rilli Valley built themselves mud huts with thatched roofs and carved a living out of the steep slopes leading down to the river meandering lazily by. The landscape and life for these people would change drastically in the summer, where temperatures could soar to over 104 degrees Fahrenheit and the monsoon rains would turn the gentle streams into raging waters. But for a few laughing children, in the month of January, this place became a beloved home away from home for a short period, and some of my fondest memories remain of joyful play, warm carefree days, and barefoot forages into the unknown.

Negotiations had been made in days gone by for the children of Dr. Graham's Homes to use the beautiful valley as a vacation spot once a year or sometimes every other year. Although my life, at times, seemed harsh and bleak, there were also wondrous and glorious days when it was anything but gloomy. What a joy it was to rise from the gloom, forget the cold, and bask in the warmth of the valley's bountiful sunshine and balmy breezes. The formidable task of moving supplies and food seven miles down the steep, rocky footpaths for sixteen children plus two staff required skilled preparations, but it always seemed to go smoothly. The results were a two-week holiday for us, with sun, sand, and happiness by the bucketful for everyone.

The first time I made the trip, I was six years old. I had to be carried in a basket perched on the back of a sure-footed Nepalese woman, one of the many local porters hired to help us make the all-day trip to the campsite. Due to the cold, I had broken out with the worst case of chilblains, large water-filled blisters on the bottoms of my feet and in between my toes, which had burst open, leading to an infection. I either had to be left behind or allow myself to be carried down on someone's back. I rebelled at this and begged to walk with everyone else. Although I stated my case for walking with the help of a friend, no amount of pleading and tears swayed the housemother.

Normally, I never gave these outbreaks another thought, knowing that I would suffer with sore feet in winter, and it never slowed me down in any way. I performed my daily duties along with everyone else, even making the trip to the dispensary on my own every day for some of Sister Cassidy's sympathy and treatment. There were others who also suffered with hard, dry, cracked feet that were also very painful, but I seemed to be most vulnerable to the blisters. While most of the other six-year-olds walked or ran down the rough paths, I was humiliated that I had to be carried down with the four- and five-year-olds, who also crouched down in baskets in order to make the trip down. I took solace in the fact, that, after two weeks of sparkling water and wading in clear pools and resting my feet, I would heal enough to be able to make the trip back on my own.

In future years to come, I wrote and talked about these trips in letters to my sponsor and mother, when I knew where she was, and my brothers and I would exchange stories with one another, for they too went on camping trips of their own during the holidays.

When the day dawned, a certain amount of excitement and anticipation was in the air. I could only think of how soon I would be outdoors, an environment I loved, and looked forward to a certain amount of freedom I was going to be gifted with. The front veranda of the cottage was a scene of bustling and chattering, as the Nepalese porters, all cheerfully speaking their own language, jostled about to take care of their little charges. Others with strong backs loaded up their designated bundles and packages of food, rice, flour, salt, sugar, tea, plastic utensils, bedding, and canvas sleeping bags, along with other necessities, to sustain us all for two weeks. Two ponies stood ready for the two housemothers, who would make the trip on horseback. They stood with sun hats and parasols, looking apprehensive and making sure everything got underway.

We were a cheery, energetic group, and soon we left the tall majestic Sal trees behind. At this time of the year, the trees were leafless and stood stark against the blue sky. In the spring, the buds would appear and mature. I loved to watch the seeds fall, as they imitated a myriad of little helicopters spiraling to the forest floor, where they would then wait for the monsoon rains to carry them off to new places. We soon stepped off the main paved road of the school grounds just below Hart Cottage and took the narrow, rocky, but well-worn path that descended gradually to the next level of the trip. It was still cold, but after a couple of miles down, we soon felt the weather start to change, getting considerably warmer. Soon we would stop for a rest and shed some of our outer clothes. Our path so far had led us past vast fields of mustard yellow millet crops, growing in abundance. The seeds from the mature plant would be ground and used for making flat, unleavened bread. Some of it was allowed to ferment to make the local alcoholic brew known as *chang* which the locals consumed in large quantities.

On our trip so far, we also witnessed tall clumps of bamboo trees, some of them with trunks six to eight inches in diameter. I remember reading about bamboo trees having hollow trunks, making them ideal for lashing yourself to in severe weather, due to their ability to bend and sway without snapping. I know that, when sliced into long strips, bamboo would be used for everything such as building strong huts, making furniture, weaving baskets and forming a drinking water system for the villages, to name a few. Our trip also brought us in close proximity to orchards of young peach and pomelo trees.

Nothing was ripe enough to eat, but without thinking, I reached out to pluck a sample. Someone passed the word along to the housemother, and as a result, I had to find the owners of the orchard and tell them what I had done. I had stolen something that did not belong to me, so it was a lesson well learned.

About halfway down on our trip, we came upon a huge banyan tree, which spread its coolness over acres of land. A small, rocky ledge had been built by local folk, and weary travelers could sit under the tree's outspread above ground root system, to renew their energy for the remainder of the trip. A welcome drink of cool, fresh water, which flowed from split bamboo pipes strapped together from high up on the hill, made the rudimentary rest stop the most ideal place for me. Here, I would sit and experience an almost spiritual feeling, especially as I looked at the small shrine to a Hindu goddess nestled in the cool shade. Most of the time, small families of monkeys would swing lazily about in the branches looking for tasty handouts from a kind passerby who happened to be making a brief stop. The sight of them hanging upside down and grabbing with their outstretched arms brought joyful laughter from us all.

As we sat in the shade waiting for the stragglers to catch up, I could feel my skin warming to the sun and my face starting to turn pink, not only from the exertion of running instead of walking down the path but also the telltale start of a sunburn that was going to be inevitable in the next two weeks. This was nothing to dwell on, and I knew that, if it got too bad, the housemother would be waiting to rub something cool on me. No sooner had the slight burning sensation begun, it was forgotten. Instead I paced impatiently, wanting to continue on to reach the camp before noon.

The porters did not stop to rest and would have already arrived at their destination, where they would be unloading their burdens and easing their backs. I didn't want to miss anything, so we started our descent to the Rilli Valley, making our way rapidly to the last landmark before sighting the camp itself. The biggest obstacle for me was the dreaded suspension bridge, built with rope and wooden slats spaced about four inches apart. The one hundred-foot-long structure, which spanned a rushing flow of water underneath, was only wide enough for a mule or horse to go across single file. When I first set eyes on this bridge, I stood frozen. I watched it sway and creak. The other end looked to be so far away. I steeled myself to look down at the huge boulders below, silently watching as the rushing water broke against their smooth sides to flow on its merry way. The sound was a roar in my ears, and I remember a dream I had over and over again of my brother Rick building something tall and imposing with his erector set, and it came crashing down on top of me. With my eyes closed and a lot of coaxing. I made it across tentatively, grasping the sides with a deathlike grip, holding my breath, and opening my eyes to step high and wide over missing slats. Over the years, I grew to love this swaying, undulating rope structure and would sometimes stand with others using our legs to make it rock and squeak by grasping the thickly woven sides.

Around the bend just after crossing over the river, our path flattened out somewhat, and we would race down the terraced paddy fields, whistling and calling out to each other as the campsite came into view. We came upon the cook huffing and puffing to get the fire going. The site of our tents, two for the girls and one for each of the aunties, was thrilling. Before I stopped to check in and make up my sleeping bag, I wanted to feel the cool water of the sparkling river between my toes. I rushed past the boulders and smooth rocks scattered amid the white sand, running straight toward the river, about a hundred yards away from the camp. This was the moment I had waited for; my exhilaration was complete. I was where I wanted to be. All other sounds faded, except for the gentle rushing of the river and buzzing of the dragonflies as they hovered over the cool pools of clear water, sipping swiftly and then soaring back up into the brilliant sunshine. I closed my eyes, spread out my arms, and turned my face up to the sky. I lifted the skirt of my summer dress and sat on a smooth, flat rock, splashing my hot, bare feet in the icy coldness and scattering the tiny minnows and crabs under the outcrops of the larger boulders that cast their shadows over the brook in places.

The sound of my name being called, brought me out of my reverie, and I jumped up quickly to make my way back to camp. Beds were neatly made up and the toiletries hidden away, and one by one, we made our way to the circle of smooth stones arranged in a circle, where we would sit and eat our meals.

The afternoons stretched before me full of adventure and promising outcomes. In our isolation, we feared nothing or no one and wandered in small groups to discover clear, blue pools to swim in. We tried to trap fish without success. No one thought of fishing poles, but at the same time, killing a fish with my own hands and eating it was out of the question. I roamed for miles, discovering small clumps of banana trees and patches of wild sweet potatoes, which I would dig up and bring back to the camp later to roast in the dying embers of the noon fire. Rare butterflies were abundant in this beautiful location, quite possibly because there were no barefoot little boys chasing after them with a net. Seeing their fleeting sips from cool streams and catching a glimpse of iridescence as they fluttered by, seemingly always in a hurry, brought vivid images of my brothers. I loved the way they recounted some of their escapades when spotting a particular species of butterfly, a blue bottle or a curry and rice, were some of the names they used to describe a specimen. I was happier here than any other place on earth. I could wander to my heart's content, disappearing from everyone's view if I wanted to. Placing my bare feet in cool waters, looking under smooth rocks for a silvery flash, collecting some of the smaller pebbles for a collection—all this and more made me forget about any infractions I may have made earlier in the day, or that consequences were waiting for me as a result.

Since we were so far down in the valley, the mornings were cold and foggy, with thick mist covering our pathway to the river. I would watch the dense, white blanket slowly rise and wouldn't see the sun come up over the tall mountain ridge until well past ten o'clock. I remember stumbling in the mist toward the sound of the river and, there, just past the break of dawn, would try to wash the sleep from my eyes with a fistful of icy water. I shivered as I tried to brush my chattering teeth without having to step foot in the rushing stream at seven in the morning, and trying to keep my tin cup from slipping through icy fingers. Until it warmed up later, we made our beds, ate our breakfast of oatmeal and bread with a steaming cup of tea, and performed a few other light household duties.

Sometimes there would be a competition between the two tents as to who had the neatest bedrolls and a treat of something like golden syrup on bread would be the reward. Prayers and Bible reading by the housemother would take place right after the morning meal, and at night when the sun went down, taking the warmth of the day with it, we would all gather around a big bonfire and sing gospel hymns and well-known songs before our bedtime. We sang in beautiful harmony that seemed to come naturally to most of us, and the villagers would venture out from their *busthees* (huts) to enjoy the music we made.

Later in the night, after I was snuggled deep inside my warm bedroll, I would silently open the tent flap and gaze at the night sky, which was something to behold. I never knew of any wild animals roaming these parts, but there must have been some. As I tried to count the stars and hoped for one of them to go streaking by so I could make a wish, the ever-present night watchman would slow his steps and come to a brief pause. In the glow of his lantern, I would see him light his rolled-up, leafy smoke, called a *birri*; take a long puff; and continue his rounds. The aroma of the strong, locally grown tobacco product filled my nostrils, and I would close the tent flap and listen to the roar of the river, which was the only sound I heard. Just before I fell asleep, I was privileged, occasionally, to hear the soft hoot of an owl calling to its mate or the raucous call of a heron, as it made its last late-night catch of fish.

After the allotted two weeks came to an end, it was with a heavy heart that I packed up to go back to the cottage, and none of us looked forward to the difficult climb back. We made our way back to the rope bridge, carrying our personal items, and after crossing its worn, wooden slats, we negotiated the steep first half of the trip back to the banyan tree. The going was not swift and exhilarating as it had been two weeks ago, and we were a silent group of stragglers, slowly ascending back up to the clouds. I walked silently, looking back often and listening for the receding sound of the river, sadder still when it was lost to view.

I felt as though the farther up I climbed, the heavier my heartfelt, for I was leaving my freedom down in the valley. While I longed to see the beautiful, snow-capped Himalayas, I also knew that I would close around myself again. The routines and hard work of our cottage life would take over in a very few hours.

For a while, and until they eventually faded, I would have my visions of the two-week holiday and would close my eyes at night to dream of iridescent butterflies and silvery fish, sunbeams and sparkling water, roasted sweet potatoes and smoky cups of hot tea. Thank you, Daddy Graham, for realizing how much this valley would mean to a little girl like me and to countless others as well. This two- week period spent in the Rilli Valley would always remain as some of the best-loved memories of my childhood.

Chapter 11

By the time I turned eleven and Mitchell was thirteen, we lost sight of our two oldest brothers, Ivan and Rick. That left Mitchell as the oldest of us four who remained at school. Rick had just turned fifteen. I remember myself at eleven trying to emulate him. He was the school's most popular boy and was known for his prowess not only on the athletic field but in the swimming pool as well. He was the topic of conversation among the teaching staff and especially the school headmaster, Mr. Scott, who had replaced Mr. Floyd. Mr. Scott, an Anglo Indian headmaster soon gained the love and respect of all the children as a stern but kind and understanding leader for our school. He did not cane any of the students as Mr. Floyd had done in his tenure there. If Mr. Scott had a favorite student, it would have been Rick, who was fearless, smart, and quick to learn.

At the awards ceremony at the end of each year, both my older brother's names were called again and again for first place, and their achievements were still visible in my later years, in the school headmaster's office, where a large plaque displayed all the first-place winners for sport and academics. When I would visit the office in my junior and senior years, I would look at those beautiful, polished wooden plaques listing the names in gold and would gaze at the name of my brother Rick, which appeared over and over again. His record set for the Harriers course (a marathon run of approximately twenty miles through rugged terrain), when he was only fourteen, a feat accomplished in bare feet, still stood in my senior year. No student had ever broken it.

I remember the day on which I first saw this race run. The senior boys of seventeen and eighteen usually ran the Harriers at the end of every school year. It was a race through the hills, up and down stony paths and steep inclines to test one's endurance. And so it was to my utter surprise and wonder that I learned that Rick was going to run for Hart Cottage. He was only thirteen at the time, a wiry little figure among the heavier, strong-looking senior runners. The captain of Hart's team had said that he needed Rick to run because of either dropouts or not enough runners for the cottage. Rick didn't hesitate. He dropped his schoolbooks right where he stood and lined up at the Jarvie Hall with the rest. I was not at the start of the race but I soon got word that my brother was running the Harriers, and right then he was spotted among the first ten runners.

I ran to the clock tower knowing that he would have to pass it on the second part of the race, and sure enough, I stood and watched with pride as he went by. He was running in tenth or eleventh place and as I looked at his face, I could tell he was enjoying himself. He flashed a grin at me as I yelled his name, and then he was gone, making another round just like the first one.

Most of the time, the runners were out of sight, due to the rugged pathways and byways they took, and we could only really see them when they came back up to the school grounds. After the first round it was hours before we saw signs of the first runner again. I couldn't tell who it was, but I knew it was not my brother; nor did I expect it to be. I thought that, by now, he would be so exhausted and fallen back or totally given up on completing the grueling race. I couldn't have been more wrong, and soon I was hearing muffled sounds of what sounded like my brother's name being relayed back to the crowd standing by. He came around Woodburn Cottage bend, up the paved road to the front of the clock tower, past the headmaster's office, and rounded the boys' playing field to the finish. He had come in second place, and not more than thirty seconds behind the leader. He was the youngest boy ever to complete the grueling course. The next year, at the age of fourteen, he not only won the race but set a record time. Several years later, Ashton would accomplish the same feat at his young age of sixteen and win the race for Hart Cottage again and again. Rick was so strong and resilient, even at that early age. He would go on throughout his life to show these strengths and never gave up his will for survival, overcoming many harsh situations and environments.

Another example came when Rick had just turned fifteen. On one particular night, just after the last of the monsoon season, ten boys from Hart Cottage made the decision to sneak out of bed at night and make their way swiftly and quietly down from the mountain to the town of Kalimpong about five miles away. Their intent was to sneak onto the Mela Ground, the town's soccer field, to watch the showing of a wonderful Indian film that would start at midnight. The city elders set up large squares of corrugated tin and covered them all with white sheets. They used this setup to show the projected film, starring Ashok Kumar, the most popular of the Indian film stars at the time, as the hero. The film, titled *Char Sou Beece*, which when translated, means 420, a term in Hindi used to describe someone who is up to some fraudulent activity, was playing all night. The movie had everything. For Rick and his friends, the songs, dances, and spectacular scenery were entertainment at the best level.

After it was over, the boys made their way back on foot in groups of twos and threes. Rick and another boy they called Lanky were the last two in, around three in the morning, and unaware of any misfortune awaiting them, they climbed through the open window of the upstairs dormitory.

Confronting them was the cottage housemother, Miss Dumont, who had been awakened by the noises the other boys had made as they'd settled into bed but witnessed only the last two boys sneaking in through the window. She advised them that she would deal with them in the morning. Rick and Lanky agreed on a story to tell, avoiding the subject of the forbidden movie escapade.

When they were questioned in the early morning hours, the boys stated that they had been out at night with their homemade slingshots, shooting down flying foxes, which were large bats that flew and swooped around at night hunting for something to eat. They each were dealt three stripes on the back of their legs with a wooden hairbrush. The two boys took this in stride and were prepared to put this one to rest and plan their next escapade.

It turned out that they never got to the first stage of planning as events unfolded and they found themselves fleeing for their lives.

That particular night of the foiled escapade, Jubilee House was broken into, and many of the contents were removed from the premises. Vases;

candlesticks; and small, valuable, shiny items were all stolen, with no sign of the thieves. Jubilee House was the residence of the principal of the school. The house was vacant at the time as the principal was on furlough, and the school secretary, was a temporary replacement although she was not occupying the residence. Her first move was to assemble all housemothers and inquire as to whether any of their boys had been out the night before, to which Miss Dumont, the Hart Cottage housemother stated that two of her boys had been caught coming in around three in the morning.

Confronting the boys, the acting principal, warned of dire consequences if she did not get at the truth. Both boys blurted out the true story of how they had gone to the movies. This new tale, combined with the original story they'd told to the housemother the night before, meant that nothing seemed to add up, and confusion set in.

Rick and Lanky couldn't turn in their friends, so they never mentioned that any other boys were out with them. Therefore, the others could not corroborate the movie escapade.

The stolen contents from Jubilee House were recovered that same day. The items had been thrown down the hillside and hidden under some dense brush not too far from the residence. Some older boys who formed a search party discovered the stolen objects, and the true thieves were never found. I vaguely remember the incident as I was only around ten or eleven years old at the time, but my brother's name was mentioned quietly in regards to a theft of Jubilee House.

I remember being looked at suspiciously and being avoided, but only by the people I cared least for. I never knew any of the details of the event at the time, and I treated it as just another obstacle to get over. I put it out of my thoughts, not realizing that I would lose all contact with my brother Rick for four unbearably long years.

Rick and Lanky knew the situation was steadily getting worse, especially when they were informed, by the housemother, that the police would be arriving the next morning to question them and force them into admitting their guilt. Neither of the boys had ever had an encounter with a policeman before, and when they were told they could go to jail, they were petrified. I know Rick would have much preferred a solid caning than to face a policeman.

The boys fled. Their feet could not touch the ground fast enough. They went to their cottage to collect whatever possessions they had, in Rick's case just a bottle of red Colgate hair oil to tame his unruly curls, and they were off on a path that was to change their lives completely. Fifteen-year-old Rick would experience a desperate and swift dash through thick jungle and unknown terrain to emerge finally on a bridge, where events that would change their lives were about to begin.

Rick and Lanky fled quickly on down from Dr. Graham's Homes' grounds using little known paths that were barely used by anyone. Fear sped them on, with Rick's sure-footedness leading the way. While their bare feet were used to the large, sharp stones and thorny bushes, they had to use all their senses to locate the right direction of the riverbank. They came to the smaller of the rivers they were looking for, the Rilli River. They followed along as far as it went, weaving in and out of the jungle. They arrived at the place where the Rilli flowed into the larger Teesta River. Rick knew they were almost at their destination, the Coronation Bridge spanning the swiftly flowing, dangerous Teesta River that tumbled straight down from the Himalayan Mountains.

The boys were about thirty miles away from their cottage by now. Rick had been on this bridge in much happier times before, on prior camping trips and treks that the boys were allowed to take on weekends. The previous excursions had just been a butterfly netting trip or exploring for wild fruits and vegetables, but now he was desperate to get as far away from the police as he could.

The Coronation Bridge, a beautiful structure built by the British in their time there, spanned the river, and once across, you could drive for miles and miles on a well-constructed road that led into the Duaars. Located in this area were huge tea plantations and bungalows surrounded by dense jungle with several villages along the way. I'm not sure if Rick had a plan to enter the Duaars or if he intended to go the opposite way, which would have led him into the train station of Siliguri sixty miles away. I think at this point they would have taken the first vehicle that stopped to pick them up, no matter which way it was headed. Children from Dr. Graham's Homes were always easily recognized in the area, as they would be young, barefoot, dressed in some type of uniform, and spoke English.

While they were on the bridge not sure of themselves or of being seen, the two boys spotted the bus coming in their direction, heading the other way leading to Siliguri. I think Rick would have rather jumped from the bridge than have to go back and face what he thought was the end of the world for him. Both boys flagged the bus down and hopped on for the short trip to Siliguri, where my brother knew he would find my mother.

When Rick and Lanky met with my mother, she grew concerned over Rick's circumstances, so she contacted Dr. Graham's Homes to ask that Rick be allowed to return and face the consequences for whatever he had done wrong. The answer, which came back by return mail, was no. She was advised that the only place left for runaway boys was a reform school in the northwest region of the Himalayas, infested with mosquitoes, wild elephants, and big man-eating cats. My mother had no other choice but to agree to the school's terms. My brother would be given a train ticket to nowhere.

The boys boarded a train northwest to the town of Bireilly, a trip which took t two days and nights. From there, they changed trains for a place called Tanikpur, about two hundred miles even further north from Bireilly. Meeting them at the remote train stop was an American man by the name of Maxton Small; his wife, Shirley; and their daughter Maxine. Mr. Small was six foot five and resembled the actor Paul Newman. Shirley resembled Debbie Reynolds, and fifteen year old Maxine was beautiful, with long blond hair, lovely blue eyes and a devastating smile, which she bestowed on young Rick. He was smitten immediately but soon realized that she was far out of his reach, and it would be two and a half years later when he was lucky enough to see her smile again.

The Tanikpur home was a self-sufficient farm-like reform school for wayward Anglo Indian boys and girls who had run away from schools, homes, or undesirable situations. From what I gathered in later talks with my brother, Rick, the farm was a product of the members of a church back in America. Through the church funds and donations from the congregation, the need arose for an institution in India to help young men and women learn skills; to help secure a place for them to grow in the church; and, in turn, to recruit other members to do God's work. Tanikpur, as the farm was called, was also associated with Dr. Graham's Homes, where children unable to graduate from Dr. Graham's would find a place to stay and work toward learning a skill. It was situated two hundred miles from the nearest big town, having just tiny villages in between and surrounded by thick, dense jungle. It would get extremely cold in the winter, being in the Himalayas, and roasting hot in the summer and monsoon months. The farm produced crops of rice, wheat, and corn; root vegetables and cabbages; potatoes, and much more. It supported the inhabitants that lived there, numbering around twenty boys and about twenty-five girls, along with a staff of about ten. Then there were the local Nepalese porters who lived in little busthees, hastily put together dwellings of thatch and mud. These locals performed various tasks, from carrying water to working on the farm itself and harvesting the food crop. When Mr. Small realized that Rick was fluent in the Nepalese dialect, he was immediately given the job of running the local dispensary, where the Nepalese servants would come every day for treatment for one malady or another.

Besides dispensing medicines, bandages, aspirin, and gentian violet, the dispensary was a stronghold for the farm's stores. There were tins of peanut butter, powdered milk, beans, cooking oil, sacks of flour, and whole wheat flour distributed to the local inhabitants, as well as lanterns and kerosene, among some of the supplies stored. The dispensary only stayed open in the winter months, the weather being too harsh for the local people to support themselves by working their crops. Rick easily made friends with everyone distributing extra food and rations to the ones most in need. He soon became a popular person on the farm, and the Small family came to rely on him more and more as the days went on. The young runaway dug into this new home and made a place for himself, soaking up every new twist and turn, learning to be self-reliant. Rick often said that this "farm" was either a blessing or a curse for the boys and girls that lived there. He used it to his full advantage and, as a result, was able to have a bearable and fulfilling experience during his four-year stay.

Ivan, on the other hand, who arrived a little later and under different circumstances, said that it was a place forgotten by God and all his angels, and he left it joyfully only a couple of months into his stay.

Rick was quick to learn, having always been interested in machinery since the erector sets of his youth. Later, at the age of seventeen, he was working the farm tractors like a professional, at the same time soaking up all the knowledge he could of how the machines worked. He became a well-liked member of the community among his peers, locals, and Mr.

Small and staff. Rick seemed to thrive here, living out his teenage years and even experiencing a little romance, although that was never allowed to blossom under the strict rules and codes of the Tanikpur farm. Mr. Small came to trust Rick in all things and placed him in work areas best suited to him, where he learned how to plow and reap with a tractor and succeeded in becoming a masterful mechanic of the best quality.

The boys and girls of the farm were watched over by a Miss Sintas, a large, strong-looking female. Not being able to venture even a glance at each other, the boys and girls formed long-distance relationships, and Maxine Small was Rick's girlfriend from a distance for at least two and a half years. If there was any infraction of the rules and a boy and girl were found to be communicating with each other, even if it was just a glance between them, the muscled men employed by Miss Sintas treated the young boy to quite a few broken bones, and he was warned never to set foot on the farm again, leaving a poor soul in the middle of a very nasty, unfriendly jungle. Meals were shared over one long table, but the boys sat on one side and the girls on the other; a large, dark curtain hung down the middle, and no one knew who was seated across from him or her. The fear of exposure to an infraction kept everyone walking on eggshells. In Rick's case, and much later into his fourth year, he found ways and means to improvise, and communications, although few and far between, were not totally impossible.

Accidents and mishaps happened numerous times on the farm. There were deaths from disease, accidents with machinery, snakebites, shootings, animal attacks, and thugs known as *dacoits* who preyed on unsuspecting individuals. No one kept any records of these incidents, as holes were dug on the outskirts and bones were buried without any kind of ceremony. In one particular incident where Rick was involved, the boys were on their way to a camp in the foothills. They came upon a two hundred-foot deep gorge spanned by a narrow, precarious, swaying bridge, the swirling water and rocks of the Sarda River directly below. The length of the structure was about twenty feet across, and it consisted of three bamboo poles, totaling about eight inches in diameter and tied together with bits of rope. One by one, Rick and a couple of the boys walked across, while some of them straddled the pole, using their hands to shuffle to the other end.

One of the boys, William, whom Rick knew very well and who was also from Dr. Graham's Homes, froze in the middle of the crossover, and no amount of coaxing and pleading could make him move even an inch. The boys would not leave him and waited for a good half hour, shouting back words of encouragement to him. William remained on the bamboo pole, unable to move, and furthermore, it looked as though he would just give up and plunge to his death. The boys talked among themselves, trying to come up with a solution and even contemplated sending someone going back across to encourage William to break the grip of fear that enveloped him.

Before they could decide what to do, Douglas, another schoolmate, volunteered to go and help talk him across. When William realized there was help within a yard of him, his hands came up, and like a drowning man, he lunged, grabbing onto his rescuer. Both boys tumbled over on the slick bamboo and were hanging onto the poles by their legs. Rick and the other boys could only stand there in utter silence. The helpless feeling they had lasted about five minutes, until, without a sound or a cry, the two boys hanging from the poles could hold on no longer and plunged to their deaths on the rocks and swiftly flowing waters of the Sarda.

Again, no record of the incident was kept. No family would enquire about the boys, and there was no one to mourn them. I heard bits and pieces of the story circulating throughout the school—two boys had drowned in a river, and Rick had gone under to find them. He could only locate one of them but could not bring the body up, as it was wedged between two large boulders. At that time I remember just being thankful that I had a strong brother somewhere and that he was not the one who'd lost his life in that harsh river.

Herds of wild elephants plagued the farm crops and destroyed everything on sight as they moved through the jungles looking for better grazing places for their ever growing family. On the boys' treks and excursions, they took tractors, trucks, guns, firecrackers, and loud noisy tin cans, all to drive the herds away. It got to the point where the elephants got used to the noises and refused to budge, because someone else had chased them away from where they had just come. On one of these trips, taken after darkness had fallen, Rick had an encounter with Mrs. Small. Shirley asked for the direction in which everyone had gone. He replied that they had all crossed the small Jugbura River. Relying on Rick's expertise, the two of them crossed over to the other side of the river in an effort o follow suit, and that's when they saw what looked like an apparition. The Nepalese have a name for this ghost that resembled a woman, dressed in a white sari that sparkled all over. She was known as a *churail*. The figure had a robust body that was covered from head to ankles by her sari; her head glowed from a light within; and her long, outstretched arms with extended fingers illuminated the ground she stood on. The most unusual features of the tall churail were the bare feet that were turned backward. A churail, it was said, would appear to lure whoever saw her into the jungle to be devoured by any number of her kind or even by the wild animals.

On their return, Rick and Mrs. Small described the encounter and the tale which would have been suspicious for its authenticity had Rick been alone, was a bit more convincing with Shirley's corroboration. Everyone knew that the ghost was out there and could send many an unsuspecting person to his or her death, so a great amount of respect was given to their tale.

Not only did people become wary of every shadow night and day, it was also a known fact that Sultan, the leader of a band of thugs known in that part of the world as dacoits, was also on the loose. During the day, the thugs prowled about like ordinary villagers looking for opportunities that would allow them to return at night and carry out their crimes of murder and theft. Along the outskirts of the fields of crops, blinds were built, made from bamboo and covered over the top by large banana leaves. Long bamboo poles used as stilts held up a small enclosure high off the ground, where there was room for just one small body and his gun. These structures were called *machans*, and Sultan aimed at spotting each and every one, as these would be the objects of his raids at night. He was looking for the guns he knew would be there.

On a dark quiet night, Rick was sitting in his machan alone hoping to capture a tiger or other large cat prevalent in the area, when Sultan visited with his band of dacoits. Fortunately, Rick's keen ears picked up the sounds of rustling movements before the group spotted his hiding place. There was not much time, and a decision had to be made. Should he climb down or jump? Rick decided climbing down was out of the question, as the rustling and movements on the machan would draw attention, so Rick opted for the jump. The fifteen-foot drop landed him on some soft sand,

and the thud gave the signal to about seven dacoits to give chase. Rick, still holding the gun in his hand, ran.

He soon outran his would-be captors and, due to his youthfulness and speed, managed to elude them. He was lucky, for quite often a boy would be left in the machan only to be found the next morning minus his gun and bleeding from wounds.

Sultan was not all bad. At times, he was like Robin Hood of old, robbing those who had and giving to those who did not. In this way, he cemented his relationship with the local villagers, who would not turn him in to the authorities.

The farm was also invaded at night by feral cattle. They ate the crops and did a lot of damage to the fields despite everyone's efforts to deter them—which included using fire crackers and firing over their heads. They soon got used to these methods of disuassion, and still continued to wreak havoc on the crops. During the day, the cattle would hang around the railway station at Bombasa, seven miles away. It was common knowledge that most of the local inhabitants were Hindu, so the cattle were worshipped and tolerated and being fed at the station. When they again wandered into the fields of crops and were becoming aggressive, the boys started firing rounds of buckshot right at them, causing some telltale signs for the locals to discover.

Once in awhile, one of the cattle would get a cartridge instead of buckshot, which led to some quick butchering in the dark and disposal of the remains before being noticed. But that still left the evidence of buckshot in the cattle, and knowing that only the boys on the farm used guns and no Hindu would hurt the cows, the locals reported the incidents to the police headquarters in the town of Haldwasi some 150 miles away.

Mr. Small got a summons from the chief inspector to answer the allegations. Rick was there and offered to go with Mr. Small, but for some reason the offer was declined. My brother was not about to give up on this trip out and advised Mr. Small that this incident could very possibly end with him spending a night or two in jail. No one would be available to drive the Chevy back to the farm. Mr. Small saw the reasoning in this and agreed to take Rick along with him.

They set off about one o'clock in the afternoon and hadn't made it very far when they came upon a very recent landslide on the road. Laborers were trying to clear the way as fast as they could, but this delayed them for about three hours, so it was six thirty in the evening before they reached police headquarters. After meeting the police chief, a portly gentleman sitting behind a large table, Mr. Small was told of the reports of cattle being fired upon and turning up injured.

"Do you know how this happened?" said the chief.

"No," said Mr. Small. "I have no idea at all, but I do need to report that we are having problems on the farm with feral cattle destroying our crops. What should we do about this?"

The police chief went into great detail about how to handle the issue, advising Mr. Small to build a fence around the farm, at which point Mr. Small stated that there were no funds available to construct a fence that would have to stretch for five miles to enclose the area. The chief asked about building a stockade and driving the cattle into it, capturing as many of them as they could. He told Mr. Small that he should then get the owners to come and collect them and ask for compensation for his damaged crops and fields. Mr. Small praised the chief for his insight and talked of how he would follow his advice.

By the time the conversation came to an end, it was approaching eight o'clock in the evening, and a long night of driving the 150 miles back looked them in the face. The chief offered to put Mr. Small and my brother up for the night and asked what they would like for dinner. After a moment's thought, Rick suggested a beef curry with *palau* rice, vegetables, and crispy *papadoms*. A night's entertainment was offered to Mr. Small, complete with the local fermented rice drink known as ruski and dancing girls, just like a story out of the legendary Scheherazade's tales of the Arabian Nights.

After they sat through a little of the entertainment offered, Max had had enough and opted for a good night's sleep instead.

When they returned to the farm the next day and rounded up all the cattle, no villagers came to rescue them, not wanting to pay for damages, so the chief of police told Mr. Small the cattle were his to do with whatever he wanted.

The cattle were loaded onto trucks and driven to the town 150 miles away, where they were turned loose never to be seen again.

Rick stayed on the farm for about six years and learned many skills that would help him in his future way of life. He learned to survive under harsh and sometimes frightening conditions. Sadly, it was because of Mr. Small's actions that he eventually had to steal away in the night and remove himself as far away as possible from the farm and the somewhat enjoyable way of life he had on the farm. He had fallen in love with Mr. Small's daughter and her with him. They were caught, and Miss Sintas's bodyguards were in full revenge mode.

Rick also found out, to his dismay, that the person in charge of the farm and the young adults residing there was leading a double life, which was successfully obscured due to the silent wall erected between the female and male inhabitants. The young women were being taken away for extended trips into the hills, on the pretense of getting away from the heat. And my brother's trust was shattered one day by the side of a secluded lake.

His presence was discovered at the same time he blundered into the secret rendezvous. Rick's fate was sealed, and he fled on foot, using his knowledge of the land and the habits of its occupants to find his way through the fierce jungle. Without rifle or knife, he made his way carefully to the village, where the local people knew him and understood the circumstances. He was very astute in the friendships he had made in his six years there, and the local village leaders helped him get away. They led him out to the railway station, where he boarded a train with their help and made his way back to Siliguri and his mother. He was just twenty years old.

Did Mrs. Small know about her husband's infidelities? She did eventually, but in a letter written to Rick after he was gone from Tanikpur, she poured out her heart to him and told him that the church back in America was saddened by her husband's sinful ways and how he had lost his way in seeking God. What started out as a place for healing and nurturing had been single-handedly destroyed by the one person trusted with the early care and guidance of so many needy young adults.

The church leaders in America closed the farm and Rick has no knowledge of its existence today.

Rick, like Ivan, found his way to Kalimpong and Dr. Graham's Homes, where Mum was now working as one of the housemothers, and it was a few short months before he was given a British subject passport and boarded a luxury liner on his way to our father in England and his future. He made his own way very quickly in his new country, using all the skills he had acquired in Tanikpur, where he married and had three children of his own.

In my talks with Rick, he seems to have fond memories of India, especially the hills in the Himalayas. He often speaks of making a trip back but has not yet. He is a great cook and speaks Nepalese often. There are some words and phrases whose true meaning can only be expressed in Nepalese. Rick is a storyteller unsurpassed by anyone, and his exciting tales of his trials and triumphs in the jungles of India, where tigers and leopards roamed freely, elephants trumpeted loudly, and thugs slithered in the night, can make his granddaughter squeal with delight. He has so much to tell, and even though I have written about some parts of his life, there is much more that I do not know. Hopefully, I will get to know it all in the very near future.

Chapter 12

My mother reentered my life when I had just turned fifteen. Other than the brief thirty minutes I'd had with her when I was eight years old, she had not been physically present in my life since I was five and had been left on the stone steps of Birissa Cottage, where she tearfully bid me good-bye. I first heard the news that she was in the area from a note I received through the housemother. The brief note was from the principal of the school and he wrote that my mother had arrived and she was staying temporarily in the isolation ward of the hospital. I was asked to pay her a visit and then report back to the principal that same day, which I did.

When I first read the news that I would be seeing her at last, I felt a sensation I could only describe as euphoria. I felt as if my body was turning into jelly and if I didn't hold on to something, I would melt away into nothingness. I know now that it was just my body letting go of most of the tension I had developed over the years. For a brief moment, I held my hand up to my heart, trying to stop the frantic beating, while at the same time, trying to collect my thoughts together. I wondered why she had not come to see me in the cottage. Why was she in the isolation ward? Was she sick?

I was still in my school uniform, a heavy, green, serge tunic with a lighter green, long-sleeve blouse under it and still barefoot, having just come in from a full day at school. I was given permission to leave immediately, and with the wind behind my back and quicksilver under my feet, I raced down the stony steps and across the girls playing field, rounded Jarvie Hall with the clock tower on top, raced at top speed along the main road, up again to the top of the church bend and past the chapel. I stopped to catch my breath briefly at the bottom of the one hundred stone steps leading straight up to the hospital and then took the steps two at a time, digging my feet into the dirt on top of them to help my stride. I soon found myself on the hospital grounds gazing up at the isolation ward.

Had my mother already seen me? I could not see her through the tiny glass windows of the outward-facing, ten-by-ten cells that reflected only darkness. After entering through the closed gate, I still had to negotiate another hundred concrete steps that started at the end of a long, glass-enclosed corridor. I flew up the steps and entered the ward. The whole trip was over a mile in distance, and I think I set a record, accomplishing it in less than a couple of minutes. It was late evening, and the light in the building was turning dark. I could hear my own footsteps and my fast breathing sounded loud but strong. The banging of the door echoed throughout the numerous empty, windowless concrete cells. Which one was she in? I ran frantically from one to the other calling out hello as I searched. I wondered fleetingly why she didn't come out to meet me, and even though it crossed my mind that she could be ill, I did not have that foreboding feeling of any kind of disaster waiting for me. I was anxious, yes, but it was not the atmosphere around me that caused me any concern for her but, rather, something else.

Could it be expectation? How would she be? Would I know her? Would she know it was me? I had kept the image of her stored in my memory all these years, and as I searched, I brought up that picture of her as I had seen her last. I remembered the beautiful, long, black hair that curled down her back; the soft, brown expressive eyes; and the full lips that hardly ever smiled. I could even remember the way she placed her feet when she walked and how my brother Ashton walked the same way.

I finally found the right cell and stood frozen in the doorway taking everything in. Her face seemed to be floating before me—still the same, still quiet, and barely smiling. She was sitting on a cot that was placed in the corner of the stone cell, and she was clasping something to her chest. All I could see from where I stood was a light-colored shawl draped across her, which fell in folds to her lap. I was ecstatic. This was *my* mother, and I wanted to reach out and touch her to make sure she wasn't a dream.

Her voice penetrated my thoughts, and she spoke my name softly as she said hello. I took slow steps toward the cot, and as I stood still in front of her, gazing at her face, I saw a slight movement of the shawl that was wrapped around her. My eyes dropped, and it was then that Mum, as we all called her, moved the shawl back to reveal what she had underneath it. I gazed upon the most angelic face I had ever seen—a tiny face with closed eyes and a fringe of dark lashes resting on each plump cheek. The small rosy mouth was relaxed in sleep, and a plump hand was grasping a baby's rattle. Dark hair lay across her tiny forehead, not curly like Mum's or mine but straight and glossy and not quite covering her tiny ears. I heard my mother's voice say that this was my sister, Sandra Shirley, and that she was going to be living in the Lucia King nursery until she was old enough to live in Birissa Cottage with me.

Could I have been any happier? I had my mother and a sister all in the same place at the same time. Mum encouraged me to take the sleeping child from her, and I didn't hesitate. I could not remember ever holding another human being in my arms before, let alone a tiny baby who was my very own sister.

Mum mentioned that Sandra was about a year plus a few months old. They had traveled up from Siliguri that day, and she was not going to leave us again. Rather, she would be staying in Dr. Graham's Homes, where she would be the junior housemother in Calcutta Cottage.

Could this be true? The hard shell around me had cracked the moment I held my sister in my arms; I had never had this feeling of belonging and such overpowering love for another human being before. I sang softly to her, "Jesus loves me. This I know." And it wasn't long before she opened her eyes and saw my face above hers. I gazed into eyes, so dark they were almost black, not soft brown like my mother's, not blue-gray like mine or my father's, and I thought how very much like Mum she was, down to the small black mole on the side of her chin. I would find out much later that she was not the child of my father, but at this time and in the coming years, my mother was the center of my world, and Sandra was her child and my sister. I couldn't have loved her more then or ever after.

I was walking on air. The feeling of being unwanted and unloved, which I had felt for so many years, suddenly seemed to disappear. Was this the total happiness that I had dreamed would one day come my way? The feeling was new and unfamiliar to me, but I rode this wave all through the rest of my school years.

Sandra was brought down from isolation and placed in the children's ward in the hospital, before joining the babies and toddlers in Lucia King. I could visit her every day after school, and she watched for me at four every afternoon. She would be standing up in her crib in her nightdress, dark eyes sparkling and the sweetest smile on her face. She knew how to sing several short hymns, which surprised me. My mother said that Rick had taught them to her when he was in Siliguri for a brief time before immigrating to England and after he fled the farm in Tanikpur. We always sang "Jesus Loves Me" before I left her every afternoon, this one being her favorite.

Before long, she was introduced into the small population in Lucia King nursery, where she would stay until she was almost five and joined me in my senior year at Birissa Cottage. All my dreams had come true. I had my mother back and a sister of my very own, who belonged to me and to whom I belonged. It was like a well- loved song that I was had been trying to compose in my head and for which I could never find the right words. My song seemed to come together now. I had found the happy ending. I had found what I loved best in the entire world. My song was in my heart, and I wrapped myself up in it. The loneliness was gone. I had someone who needed me. I had my mother. I never wanted to be parted from my mother and sister again.

My mother took up her housemother duties in Calcutta Cottage, which housed thirty-two boys ranging in age from four to eighteen. I can picture her standing in the back doorway of the cottage every morning so she could get a glimpse of me on my way to the chapel at the start of the school day. The cottage was located closest to the school and church, and the road would rise up on an incline before forming a steep bend to the left, where one could stop and look down on the cottage itself.

Even though I did not have my mother in my cottage life, I could wave to her every day and know that she was just five minutes away from anything and any place in our little community. I would visit her on weekends and on her days off, and we would take long, quiet walks in the nearby woods and hills. I hardly spoke of my father to her, except to ask if she had heard from him. I still had not realized that he was pretty much gone from our lives at this point. I think I just refused to believe that this was possible.

My younger brothers hardly knew of his existence, and they never posed any questions about him. Once a month, Mum would take Ashton, Julian, and me into the town of Kalimpong to experience the sights and sounds of this bustling, busy marketplace. We would eat a meal of curry and rice or a plate of Chinese *momos* in the local restaurant, and little Julian's eyes would get big and round. We made the trip down on foot and negotiated the price of a ride in a jeep back up the mountain with a Nepalese driver. I give much credit to the kindness of the principal of Dr. Graham's Homes, for stretching out his hand to my mother when she needed it again. She had always had a purpose in her life—was always moving toward the ability to be with her children again—and even though it took her several years, with the help of Dr. Graham's again, she was able to accomplish this.

That year flew by, and I swept the awards for track-and-field events, swimming, and diving, even being the first to fly off the diving board in a backward swan dive, something I'd taught myself to do. My mother was my inspiration, and I would give her all the awards and watch as the lovely smile would appear on her face. I knew she was proud, even though she never uttered the words.

She made new friends among the younger Anglo Indian staff and Indian teachers and grew more beautiful every time I saw her. She was able to spend her days off from work in whatever way she wanted to. She usually had every other Friday and Sunday off, and some of her happier days were spent exploring the movie theaters and restaurants in the town of Kalimpong, with occasional trips to Darjeeling, which was much more cosmopolitan and had a large Anglo Indian population as well.

The year ended on a high note for me, and I did not experience the dread I usually did when the Christmas holidays came around. I knew that I would be together with our little family, and mother would make her steamed Christmas pudding, in which she inserted coins. My siblings would have a wonderful time searching through their portions for the one, fifty *anna* (Indian coin) piece that would be the envy of all. We could buy a whole shop full of sweets with that much money, my favorite being *ghur buns* (a dark, pure cane sugar delight) a treat we all loved.

My brother Mitchell, who had left Dr. Graham's Homes by now, was waiting in the Birkmyre Hostel in Calcutta for his British traveling documents to come through, and Rick and Ivan had already taken the long trip across the ocean to England. It would be almost seven years before I would see them again. At this time, I thought only of the happiness that had at last come to me, and nothing was going to let the past swim to the surface of my mind.

Chapter 13

At the end of the first year with my mother back in my life, my name appeared on "the list" for the first time. There was no need to rush down the hill to the post office and pretend to look for my name. My siblings and I were going to be on a train like everyone else, and we would join our mother for a Christmas holiday away from Dr. Graham's Homes. This was to be our first vacation together as a family. Mum had arranged for us to travel to Shillong, a beautiful hillside town in the northeast province of Assam. Included in our little entourage were my brothers Ashton and Julian, Sandra, our mother, and myself. We traveled the two days and a night by train and arrived at a home owned by an Anglo Indian relative of an acquaintance of my mother's.

The home in which we were to spend the next two months, had two separate living quarters. While our hosts lived in the main building, my mother soon had us settled quite comfortably in to the guest quarters. The people of Shillong spoke a language called Khasi, which was totally unfamiliar to me, and they dressed differently as well. We had some schoolchildren who were from Shillong at Dr. Graham's Homes, and though they preferred to associate with each other more than the rest, I made friends with one or two. Here too, as in the Duaars and Darjeeling tea estates, the British had had a huge influence, and the Anglo Indian population was widespread, with children being born and leaving their Indian mothers to become borders at Dr. Graham's Homes.

At sixteen, I was extremely uncomfortable in my own skin. Not pretty by any means and plagued with some unwelcome teenage skin conditions,

I lacked a certain amount of self-confidence and rather than interact with new acquaintances, I would sneak away on my own to read a book or sit in the primitive little kitchen on a small, three-legged stool and watch my mother prepare the evening meals. Sometimes she would cook, but most of the time, she hired a local girl who cooked for us and helped keep the living area clean.

I learned so much that holiday. For instance, there were a hundred different types of rice, identified by the region each variety grew in, as well as its shape, length, texture, color, and aroma. Up until this time, I had only known of the brownish rice we ate in school and which, compared to what my mother cooked, had no taste or aroma. I learned about spices, using both the Nepali and English names, and the importance of only choosing the freshest to be ground and made into a paste before actually going into the pot to be cooked with meat and vegetables. I was ecstatic to learn that curries could be cooked in a hundred different ways, and bitter greens, which I disliked so much in school, could be made to melt in your mouth with a burst of flavors like I never knew existed. Even today, when I cook a pot of basmati rice, and the first waft of its aroma arises, I feel so very close to my mother and family and reminisce on the times when I would learn from her as we prepared our evening meals in the primitive but cozy and warm kitchen.

Every Christmas in Shillong, the weather would become extremely harsh, with cold winds blasting down the mountains and temperatures dropping to freezing. While the winters in Dr. Graham's Homes were quite mild in comparison, Assam was more exposed to the harsher weather on the northeast side of India. Living spaces in Shillong were only heated by a fireplace in the bedroom, which had to be lit as soon as the sun went down. Mother had saved what she could of her small salary to give us this holiday, and to me, it was heaven. We were together, and I never felt the extreme cold or worried about the lack of warmer clothes to wear.

Sitting outside one especially rare and beautiful sunny morning, I heard the soft strumming of a guitar. Looking around to locate the direction of the sound, I heard a voice say, "Hello!"

I could see nothing or no one, but then the voice said in broken English, "Up here please."

I looked up, and there on the roof was the guitar player, grinning down at me. I could tell that he was several years older than me, with short, spiky, black hair; smooth, olive skin; and a row of perfectly nice teeth. I felt glued to the rock I was sitting on, and I knew I was turning red from the roots of my blond, watered-down curls to the toes in my too tight shoes. Aside from the brief encounter several years ago with the boy who had grabbed me by the neck in an effort to kiss me, I had never spoken to any boy apart from my brothers. A side glance now and then was all I would allow myself. Tiny beads of sweat popped up on my nose. I wanted no part of this conversation; all I wanted was to disappear into the ground.

My mother was in the background somewhere, because the boy then greeted my mother respectfully, calling her by name. I heard her murmur a greeting back, and she entered the door that led back into the house.

He asked for my name, and when I told him, he tried to repeat it and totally missed the pronunciation at first. Later, after some coaching, he came up with a name that was quite satisfactory to me. I learned his name was Jimmy, and he was the youngest son of our hosts. I spent one of the happiest months of my entire life so far, mostly in the company of my newfound friend.

That winter of turning sixteen, I kissed a boy for the first time, which was quite pleasant, and I learned to look him in the eye, not worrying about my too curly hair, too white sometimes blotchy skin, or ill-fitting hand-me-down clothes. A gentleman in every way, Jimmy taught me how to play three chords on the guitar and sing with him soft little songs and catchy tunes. He was blessed with a truly lovely voice—not a loud, strong baritone but, rather, a husky, soothing tenor—and when he sang and strummed his guitar, all ears stopped to listen. I learned to speak some Khasi, and I, in turn, read some of my books to him. He was never happier than seeing me dressed in the fashion of his race, and I loved putting on the warm shawls and tying them over my shoulder just like his older sisters did.

I often dwell on what I know now to be the sweet innocence of his and my youth, never going beyond more than just soft kisses and holding hands. My mother watched, never saying a word. She didn't encourage or discourage me, and I was always by her side, except on some cold afternoons when Jimmy and I, wrapped up in blankets, would sit on the roof and sing, softly strumming the guitar. He didn't speak very much

English, but music was all we needed. I didn't like conversation anyway, so this was as perfect as it could get for me.

I especially loved the long walks we would take, with both families going further up into the hills, gathering walnuts and wild winterberries. We would carry the means to make a fire and boil the fresh water from a spring to make our hot cups of sweet tea, and I was at peace with love around me.

My idyllic holiday was shattered when it came to an abrupt ending one cold and gloomy afternoon. My mother, brothers, sister, and I were in the open market buying much-needed supplies of food and oil. My mother had said that she had a little extra money and asked if I would like to have a piece of fabric for a dress to be made for me. I was ecstatic—my very own first new dress—and I chose a lovely sheer organza that she said turned my eyes the color of turquoise. It had gold flecks sparkling all over it, and I knew that I wanted a grown-up dress to be made, with straps on my shoulders.

Mum paid for the fabric and I watched as she put her wallet away into the inner pocket on the inside of her short green coat. I was cradling my beautiful new purchase that was wrapped up in brown paper and tied with string. My thoughts were on the beautiful new dress I was going to wear, so I was not fully aware of the crowd bustling around our tight little group. After making sure that all of us were together, my mother turned, and with Sandra's little hand held tight in hers, my brothers and I turned to follow her away from the fabric stall. I vaguely sensed a brief moment of increased jostling and the crowd seemed to close in on us slightly. I felt hemmed in, but then in the next instant I suddenly felt free from the mass of shoppers around me. It was at this moment that I heard my mother's frantic voice calling out to me saying that she had been robbed. I looked around at the sea of faces before me hoping to find some clue as to who would have stolen from my mother, but the crowd of shawl clad people around me were either going on about their business or looking at us with curiosity. Every rupee she possessed—which she had saved throughout the year—was gone. We turned the coat inside out. There was nothing. We searched the area we were standing in and tried to retrace our steps. I was still hoping that a miracle would happen and we would find the money in another place hidden in her coat, or perhaps in the stall where we had purchased the fabric, and I was not yet willing to accept that the money by now was gone forever. Neither the wallet nor the money ever turned up, and I could see my mother's face crumble as she realized that what had just happened would put an end our first holiday together.

We walked back from the market in silence, and I somehow felt that I should have been able to prevent this. Perhaps if I had been more vigilant and not wrapped up in my purchase of the beautiful fabric, I might have been able to do something or might have seen how it had happened. I was as devastated as Mum was, especially when she told me that we would have to pack up our things and head back to Dr. Graham's Homes. Luckily, she had purchased return trip tickets for the train ahead of time, so we packed as much food as we could for the trip back, so as not to have to purchase anything on the way. I took a tearful leave of Jimmy, telling him not to write any letters in his broken English, as they would only be read by the housemother and I would not get them anyway. I left, telling him I would return again next year, but I never did. His memory was a place in my heart, staying there for many years to come.

I saw Jimmy one more time when I had just turned twenty-one and he was a little older, married, with a beautiful wife and children. I was a teacher at Dr. Graham's Homes by then. Through his younger sister, I learned he was in Siliguri, some sixty miles away, and was asking my permission to come and visit. I thought this over for a long time before I admitted to myself that I wanted to see him again, to thank him for accepting me in all my awkwardness and insecurity, to tell him he made me feel beautiful for the first time in my life, so many years ago in that one brief month of my sixteenth year. I wanted to know if he had changed and what he was doing with his life. I know I had changed tremendously.

I was somewhat more at ease with myself, although I still had a long way to go. I had experienced a few relationships, some good ones and some not. Gone were the blotchy skin and too tight curls. I wore lipstick now, my hair was swept up in a fashionable French twist, and I was almost five foot six and wearing high heels. Yes, physically I had changed, but I was still too shy and quiet and unsure of what, if anything, to say next.

When we were face-to-face again, I was taller than him, but the dear face had not changed at all. He was now the shy one, still speaking very little English. We soon slipped into the familiar soft conversations we used to have; after all, he had once been so dear to me. We looked at pictures of his family, and I felt that he was the one who was now so secure in his own little world.

The almond-shaped eyes filled up with tears when we said our good-byes, and as he held my perfectly manicured fingers in his rough hands, I could not hold back my tears either. We knew we would never see each other again, but I wished with all my heart that he would know of my gratitude for the joy and happiness his friendship brought me so many years ago. He'd noticed me and reached out his hand and heart for me to hold on to. I can never look at a guitar player without seeing Jimmy and the gentle sweet soul that he was.

Chapter 14

After the robbery, I don't remember much of the trip back to Dr. Graham's Homes. My thoughts were full of Jimmy and my shattered holiday. I was heading back to drudgery. Sandra would go back to Lucia King. Ashton and Julian returned to Hart or Assam Cottage. I didn't know or care where I ended up. We still had a month before all the kids would be back from their holidays to start the school year again, and I dreaded having to explain to my enemies why I hadn't completed my holiday. I felt as though I had failed at protecting my family, and only the memories of Jimmy sustained me. My mother was at a dreadfully low point in her life again, and I didn't know how to cheer her up, so I stayed away and rarely saw her as she took up duties again in a cottage.

I finished out the rest of the holidays as a nurse's helper at the hospital. I was back to scrubbing floors and cleaning out toilets and making the trip every day, twice a day two miles to the post office and back, carrying the heavy leather bags of mail.

Life went on as always and soon all the vacationing kids were back. The new arrivals were processed for diseases and immunizations, which took several weeks to accomplish, all while living in the cells of the isolation ward. Each cottage would get one or two new children to assimilate into the cottage and school life, and it was always quite nice to get to meet and learn about them. I processed myself as well, soon becoming involved once again in my studies and daily routines, only taking on even more responsibility than before. I tucked Jimmy away into a corner of my heart to take out at night before I went to sleep. Even this precious memory would fade, and along with all the conflicting thoughts and feelings going on in my head and body, I would come to call upon my heart less and less.

I realized that, the older I became, responsibilities for me, both in the cottage and within my family took immediate priority. That was never more prominent than in the middle of my sixteenth year, when my mother took a fall and was hit in the back of her head by a punching bag at the gym. She was unconscious for a while and suffered a very bad concussion. The head injury led to her admission into the hospital, and I was able to visit her often. It was a month before she was released.

I was summoned to the office of the principal and was asked in a kind way about my mother's welfare. I inquired why he'd asked the question, and he told me that Mum was suffering from severe depression, and he thought I might be able to shed some light on the reason. Not knowing much about my parents' marriage situation at the time, I could only think of the recent holiday cut short by robbery. I also realized that both her eldest sons, Ivan and Rick, twenty-one and nineteen years old respectively, had left for England within months of each other that same year, and in a conversation with her, she conveyed to me that she quite possibly would never see them again. It was almost twenty years before she did see them again. At that time they were well into their own married lives, with children of their own.

I was asked by the principal to speak to my mother's friends and solicit their help. I tried to do everything in my power as well to get her through this difficult time. I threw myself into everything, becoming competitive and striving to win all the awards both individual and team, thinking that this would help give her a spark of interest in her life once again. Yes she would smile, but her eyes never said anything.

I would realize later that my mother never let her emotions surface, preferring instead to withdraw and to block out what she didn't want to face, protecting herself and her mind. I was learning from her how this was done and became like her in that respect. It took me half my life, and a distance of two whole continents, to understand the workings of positive thinking and that happiness is within us all, but only if we let ourselves be less inhibited by the past.

By the end of that year, just before I turned seventeen, I experienced popularity on the field of sports and earned the admiration and respect of many of the teachers. I had been an average student, but I was starting to take my studies a little more seriously now and began to improve my grades.

My renewed interest was partially, or even mostly, attributable to a wonderful new South Indian teacher by the name of Mr. Bernard T. Brooks. He took our minds to places I didn't know existed and taught us how to think for ourselves and question everything. Previously in our curriculum, we'd never had an anatomy class and were somewhat naive in regards to the workings of the human body. Our teacher was young and recently married to my fourth-grade teacher, and, yes, we all thought he was handsome. So it was that I first learned at the age of seventeen how the human body was put together and how it functioned and existed. Up until then, our quiet whispering to each other, the growing awareness and curiosity of our own bodies, and a stolen book with a love story was the extent of my knowledge. Our education on this subject with Mr. Brooks was professional on every level, and I am ever grateful for his insight.

The one regret I have is not having parents there to ask about the other facts of life, such as diseases, different lifestyles, contraception, and the like. We only knew that everyone had to be married, and having children under any other circumstances was a disgrace. No one ever got pregnant or expelled from school due to a pregnancy or clandestine affair.

While I learned a few details to further my sex education from my more knowledgeable college friends, I still had a lot to learn on my own and brought myself kicking and screaming into reality some years later. It was preferable that only the girls sign up for the biology class, so with the absence of our boy classmates, we were free to ask our questions without giggles or nudging or immature smirks common among teenagers. The boys were off doing science projects or learning about tools, so when we initially got over our introductions to Mr. Brooks, the seven girls in his class, over time, were led skillfully and willingly, into the world of reproduction and human anatomy. I for one was enraptured of the way he not only taught us but learned from us as well. He did not stand there and ask us questions but, rather, noticing our hesitancy, he skillfully elicited from us what little knowledge we had of anything. We were naive enough to ask questions we'd all wondered about but had never asked anyone, and in the end, the lessons became conversations and understanding of subjects that had been closed to us. I was lucky enough to be in the first class ever taught by this man in our school, and he went on to become, first headmaster and then principal of Dr. Graham's Homes, going down in its history as one of the most beloved of all teachers in the school. He was the first Indian principal of Dr. Graham's Homes, a position well deserved and it was an honor to have been one of his first pupils.

I experienced two great years with Mr. Brooks and went on to excel in biology and passed with a good grade in the final exams. He made a big impact on my young life then and even after. When I went back to teach at my old school, he had been promoted to headmaster. I glimpsed through him what confidence and knowledge could do for me, and he gave me belief in myself.

I was on the school hockey and basketball teams, even though I was not a senior, which allowed me to travel with the older girls to interschool competitions. We excelled just by sheer will and courage, still playing out everything in our bare feet. There was not much knowledge of technique, and coaches were unheard of. It may have been quite possible that the convents and private schools we competed against were informed that we were going to be different since we wore no shoes and played in strange-looking sports outfits. They never laughed at us or made any remarks, at least not to our faces, so we never had to defend our appearance to anyone. Besides, the trophies we carried back with us took over all other conversations. I was growing tall and strong and could defend my smaller team players with a strength of will and spirit. I was elected junior prefect of the girls, an honor given to students who were chosen by the staff and their peers. This group of eight, which included a captain, vice captain, and six prefects, wore navy blue blazers with the school emblem embroidered on the pocket. We organized all school functions and worked closely with the school staff. I considered being chosen a high honor and took my duties seriously. In my last two years, I was voted senior prefect first and vice captain after that and awarded the Mountbatten Cup for the best student of the year.

Everything seemed so far removed from the beginning of the year. The robbery incident had almost faded from memory, but not Jimmy. I still hoped I would see him again, although I was resigning myself slowly to the fact that our reunion anytime in the near future was going to be impossible. Like everyone else I cared about in my life, he was gone, and I would give him up to being just a memory.

I hope Mr. Brooks, wherever he is in his beloved India, comes across this book of mine and remembers me. I think about the photographs he took of us for our first school magazine under his watch and how he lamented the fact that he could never get me to smile. When I think of him, which is often these days, I smile.

Chapter 15

I turned seventeen that December, and this time, my mother arranged a Christmas holiday in Calcutta for all of us. It was very exciting, as we knew so much about this popular city from the school kids who lived in or near it. I remembered Calcutta from my prior holiday visit when I was fourteen. I also learned that, at the end of this school year, my mother would not be returning to Dr. Graham's Homes and was looking for employment elsewhere. I had one more year to go before I sat for my final exams, so I would be returning to school without my mother. This time, though, I would know where she was and would never lose contact with her again.

The holiday started out full of promise. Unfortunately, it turned out to be quite the opposite. We were part of a group from Dr. Graham's Homes going to live in the home of a married couple; the wife was Anglo Indian, and the husband was from South India. They had advertised reasonable rates and good accommodations for families. I don't know what my mother paid them for our stay, but my brothers, sister, mother and myself, found ourselves confined to one room, where we slept on the floor in an upstairs "flat," with no room to turn over in bed. I took this in stride. I had slept on the floor before, and this wouldn't be the last time. There was no running water, and the facilities were very basic. I especially dreaded using the toilet facility at night. When I switched the light on, the scurrying of a dozen or more, huge, flying cockroaches would be enough to send me to bed without washing or brushing my teeth. Oddly enough, none of us complained. I had been through rough times before but couldn't help hoping that my mother hadn't paid everything she had to this couple, thinking that we were going to get a better place.

Every meal had to be purchased from the street vendors, and there were an abundance of various entrepreneurs calling out their wares. We got accustomed to eating from these outdoor cookers, and the food was always cheap and tasty. The thought of any aftereffects on our stomachs never entered our heads.

My two younger brothers, who were teenagers by now, were allowed to explore their surroundings and meet up with our third brother, Mitchell, who was older than me by about a year and a half. He had left school at the age of seventeen to seek employment in Calcutta and was staying with other boys from Dr. Graham's Homes in a hostel that had been set up by Daddy Graham when he was still alive. Here the older boys who did not sit for final exams could spend their time waiting for a passport to the United Kingdom or work in the bakery or ice cream shop run by Dr. Graham's Homes.

Mitchell stayed in the Birkmyre Hostel for three years before my father sent for him, and he received the necessary documents to travel to England. I adored all of my brothers, but Mitchell and I were exceptionally close all throughout school. I wanted only to please him and make him happy, and there were no lengths I wouldn't go through to accomplish this. Even today, we are still very close. We know each other's faults. We had our ups and downs, our highs and lows, our good times and bad. We went through times when we weren't on speaking terms, and on other occasions, we were inseparable when we were together.

He was heartbreakingly handsome, with eyes as blue as the sky on a clear day, fringed with long, dark eyelashes; a square jaw; perfect skin and teeth; and glistening, black hair. I still tease him today about all the languishing females he left behind, not only at our school but also at some of the other school, even as far away as Calcutta. With all his good looks, Mitchell was extremely shy and unaware of the hearts he was breaking. I can only remember one girl who stole his heart. She was from Bene Cottage, and she and I became good friends until she left school early to move back with her parents. It was a long time before my brother experienced a lasting relationship with a girl again.

On this particular holiday, I was able to catch up with my brother and see him from time to time. My two younger brothers would run across him more often, and the three spent much-needed brother time together. Sometimes at night, I would climb the stairs to the roof of the flat and look out over the Calcutta skyline. The bright neon sign of the Brook Bond Tea Company fascinated me and was a landmark that was clearly visible as you entered the city. I would gaze at the green teapot pouring tea into the red cup and saucer and watch as it flashed on and off all night long. I could hear the sound of the Muslims being called to prayers, and at the same time, I could hear the beating of the *thablas* as the Hindus danced and made offerings to their temple gods.

The sounds and smells of India became a large part of my life and still linger in my mind, heart, and soul. I would look down onto the street below me and see life going on, where something was happening every minute of the day. I would hear the jangling bells of the rickshaw as the runner looked for a client and see the overhead awning of his two-wheeled carriage covered in flowers and bright garlands as he moved into line with the other owners of similar forms of transport. The fragrant aroma of the spices being cooked on the street wafted up on the gentle night wind. Evening trips to the New Market by rickshaw took us to the very center of the city, and the lights, noises, and smells were overpowering and enduring.

The entrance to the New Market, one of my favorite places, had hundreds of stalls jammed up against each other. I immediately became aware of the fragrances of exotic flowers that were strung into garlands or woven into intricately elaborate hair ornaments to adorn a bride's head. As you moved farther into the brightly lit market, stall after stall would display cascading samples of delicate silk saris in every color imaginable. The gold and silver threads passing through them looked like liquid ribbons. When I rounded a corner, I would be in a world of sparkling gems consisting of rubies, sapphires, and emeralds, and if that didn't stop you in your tracks, then the very next brightly lit stall with its tiger and leopard skin rugs would. This stall was popular with the European and Western customers. The intricately carved chests and tables inlaid with ivory could be shipped to homes as far away as America at the buyer's request. This vibrant market and its inhabitants held me in its spell every time I visited there and became a glowing memory that would remain with me all of my life. Six years later, while strolling through the brightly lit stalls, I would first set eyes on my future husband.

In many ways, this holiday in Calcutta opened up my world and my eyes. I experienced different kinds of music, met Anglo Indians at every turn, and even glimpsed another side of adult life. Since it was the Christmas holiday, Dr. Graham's Homes' boys and girls inhabited the popular places in the city. It wasn't difficult to find someone if you wanted to. I particularly favored Firpos, the chocolate shop, and would run into many people I knew. During lunchtime, I would stroll into Mocambos for a bowl of spicy mulligatawny soup, made with red lentils and lamb. It was said to have been an Anglo Indian concoction put together to please the British palate.

During this holiday, I was contacted by an older man who said he knew my father and had even seen me as a tiny baby. He specifically sought me out because, even in the big city of Calcutta, word spread quickly as to who was in town and where he or she could be found. The man mentioned that he had been a friend of my father's, and I agreed to talk more while sitting down to tea with him.

When I mentioned this man to my mother, I witnessed for the first time, a sense of something like panic and agitation in her. I was puzzled at her reaction and even more so when she asked me not to continue seeing him. I had been taken in by his kindness and his mention of being my father's friend. I was still keen for any word of my father, and it showed all over my face when his name came up. I never found out what the man's intentions were. I still would not ask questions of my mother. But whatever it was she had stored up in her mind about their past, I was intuitive enough to know it must not have been good, and she wanted to protect me from it.

I still looked to my mother for guidance and didn't want to displease her in any way. Being seventeen was exciting, but I was also hesitant and apprehensive of the unknown. I was given a little freedom of my own for the first time, and Mitchell came to my rescue once or twice when I would have been taken in by a kind voice or a sweet word. He knew everyone in the city, having already been a resident for three years. He backed up my mother in her dislike of the older gentleman and saw to it, with just a few words to him, that his sister would not be available for afternoon tea again. There had to be a lesson here for me, and though I did learn from it, that didn't stop me from making the wrong choices along with the good in the future years to come.

My mother scoured the local paper every day, looking through the want ads for a position she could apply for. One day, she was lucky enough to find something that looked promising. She quickly went to the public telephone booth and made the call. An interview was set up immediately for the next day in a room at the Grand Hotel, and my mother looked pleased and happy as she readied herself. We all went along with her, upon the request of the person conducting the interview. We put on our best "going out" clothes and waited for our mother to finish. She looked lovely in her deep, rose-colored top and navy blue skirt, and I prayed with all my heart that this would be a happy occasion for her. We walked out into the warm sunshine, where my mother hailed a taxi for the trip. We usually walked whenever we went anywhere, not wanting to spend the funds on a ride when we had two perfectly good legs to get us there, but this was special and she wanted to arrive in style.

Even with all of us crammed into the back seat, the ride was stupendous. I had never seen a traffic light before, and there was one set up on Park Street. It took me a while to figure out how the cars didn't all crash into each other at the crossroads. Other than that particular traffic light on that street, traffic rules were nonexistent, and it was a race wide open for the bravest and the fastest. We squealed and laughed at all the antics going on as we narrowly missed a bicycle or a rickshaw, and the driver got caught up in our enthusiasm, showing us how he could slip by an unsuspecting taxi driver, at the same time avoiding a cow placidly chewing his cud in the middle of everything. It was fascinating to see how polite the taxi drivers were to each other, nodding their heads and waving their arms around, all the while using some undesirable language under their breath as bolder drivers flashed by in an unbelievably narrow opening in the traffic.

We made it to the Grand Hotel in time, and what a sight it was. It was a grand structure indeed, with marble columns holding up a domed entryway, complete with nodding waiters and bearers. They were dressed in white Indian pajamas and tunics with colorful turbans on their heads. We were impressed as we silently followed our mother into the hotel, our mouths wide open in awe at all the paintings and tapestry on the walls and the brocade-covered furniture sitting on the gleaming, marble floors. We were led up rich, red-carpeted stairs to a sitting room all laid out with tea and pastries, from Firpos no less.

It wasn't long before I heard a booming voice, and in walked a very large, middle-age woman, with short gray hair, dressed in a gray suit and low heeled shoes. Her cheery hello to us all helped ease my mother, and she smiled slightly. The rest of us just stood there with our mouths open and eyes wide. My immediate thought was, *Is this person a man or a woman?* I thought my mother had said that she was being interviewed by a Miss Balantine. I guess the severe haircut, the booming voice, the penetrating gray eyes, and the dark shadow of hair above her top lip made me blink in surprise. Despite this first impression, the moment she turned her attention to Mary's children standing there in silence, she would become another beloved figure in my future life.

As we ate our lovely cakes and drank tea with sugar and cream, trying not to act like we hadn't eaten in weeks, not speaking unless spoken to, and striving not to let the crumbs escape our fingers, Miss Balantine conversed with our mother. Needless to say, in a very few minutes, we had politely eaten our way through a dozen cream cakes and finished off all the square lumps of sugar from the sugar bowl.

We soon found out, not long after that meeting, that my mother was immediately hired for the job of housemother to about five hundred girls in Dow Hill School, a private and exclusive school in the hilltop town of Kurseong, a place my mother was very familiar with. She had been allotted a good salary and a private room and bathroom of her own in the senior girls' dormitory. She would not only supervise the senior girls, but would later be promoted to director of School Food Services for the entire school. For this, she would be given a private home on the premises as long as she was employed there and would have her own household employees.

My mother spoke fluent Nepalese, and this would help her become indispensable to Miss Balantine, who gave her the keys to the supply rooms. In addition to organizing the food and distribution of supplies, my mother was in charge of hiring local folk to work in the kitchens and on the school grounds. In the end, my mother became a truly valuable member of the headmistress's staff and earned the respect of all the local Nepalese people for her stern but fair way of handling all their disputes and grievances.

A couple of years later, on leave from my studies in Poona, where I attended St. Mary's Training College for teaching, I returned to Kurseong for a brief break and ran into Miss Balantine at my mother's cottage. She had taken to having tea with my mother in the afternoon, and sure enough, the booming voice calling out "Esther" (as she liked to call my mother) fell on my ears, a familiar sound of my past. I was no longer the young, shy less-than-confident girl of seventeen I'd been when we had first met but already had a year of university behind me. She naturally took up the subject of my studies. We went on to become good friends. I spent many a winter afternoon sitting by her huge, warm fire, drinking hot cocoa, eating biscuits, and discussing everything from earthworms mating to the classics of Pearl S. Buck, poems by Browning, and the writings of Rabindranath Tagore. I had a fondness for this lady, which came as a big surprise to me. I was especially glad for the way I felt at ease in her company, where I could discuss anything on my mind. I loved that she opened up her library to me on those short, dark winter afternoons, and I always remember her with love and respect, holding her in the highest regard.

My mother made a home for herself here and for her children who remained in India, and when she retired many years later, it was only then that she showed any signs of desire to leave her mountaintop home to join me and my family in America.

Chapter 16

I had one more year left at Dr. Graham's Homes, my graduation year. Together with Ashton and Julian and Sandra, now four years old, we parted from our mother in Calcutta after the Christmas holiday was over. We found our way to the train station and made the long, two-day trip back to school. My mother took up her new position in Dow Hill School at the beginning of March, and we looked forward to spending the Christmas holidays with her at the end of the school year. In my senior year, my best friend Sarah was elected Captain of the school and I was the Vice Captain. Between us and the prefects, we did our best to make it a good year for all. During this year, my sister Sandra left the Lucia King Cottage for toddlers and babies, and joined me in Birisssa Cottage where life began for her as it did for all of us, performing small duties and going to school. It was my responsibility to care for her and dress her for school every morning, making sure she was ready for the day, with neatly combed hair and clean face and hands. As I performed all my tasks, I listened for her voice and chatter, and I came running if I heard the smallest cry of discomfort, where I dried her tears, smoothed back her hair, and let her know that she always had me close by.

Sandra, in turn, became my constant shadow, slowly but surely growing accustomed to the daily routine. Unlike me, she became quite a pet with the housemother and teacher in charge of our cottage. Never having been taken under anyone's wing and not bonding easily with girls my age or older authority figures for any length of time, I sought to let my sister know right from the start that I would be there for her no matter what.

At night, when the weather turned very cold, I would crawl exhausted into my bed after a long day and night of doing chores and studying for my final exams. Almost always, I would encounter Sandra's little form under my blanket at the foot of my bed and my cold sheets unexpectedly warm as toast. After she was tucked in for the night, she would move over to my bed, which was always beside hers and situated at the entrance to the dorm. Sandra made sure she left a hump in the middle of her own vacant bed before crawling into mine. Sometimes, I would cuddle her before putting her back in her own bed, where I would also find the Siamese cat Ching curled in a ball under the covers. I was thankful for my sister's presence in my life that final year. She endeared herself to many with her sunny nature, and I had the love of a child—a kind of love I had never known before.

The last year of cottage life proved to be difficult and challenging. I was the only senior in my cottage who was sitting for the finals, and while the other two or three older girls were looking at becoming nurses' aides and nursery helpers, I had chosen to go on with my studies and further my education if I was successful in passing the tough final exams. We sat for the finals, administered by Cambridge University in line with other European school curriculums. The housemother of Birissa Cottage at the time was a missionary from Scotland. And while she was not as harsh—somewhat softer in her approach to the children in her charge—as some of her predecessors, she still expected a lot from me. She put me in charge of teaching the younger girls how to scrub out toilets and slimy drains, making it sound as if I was the only one who knew how to get the job done.

The oldest girl in the cottage, a redhead older than me by five months, seemed to get away with lighter duties, if she performed any at all, and had long given up on attending classes at school, waiting instead for her immigration papers to Australia. So between the scrubbing and trying to study, I felt overwhelmed and drew back further and further behind the wall I had put up around me. I never spoke to the housemother much, and if the question of how my preparation for the exams was going came up, I gave her a curt answer and took my books with me to find a quieter spot down the hillside or in the treetops, where I studied and dreamed of my future.

About halfway through the school year, word got out that the two senior girls from Mansfield Cottage were allowed to bypass all their duties and concentrate only on their school studies. Their housemother was always promoting "her girls," and she gave them free rein to come and go pretty much as they pleased. She spoke of their prowess so much that my housemother, not to be outdone, informed me that I would no longer be required to perform any of my daily duties. She wanted me to be able to spend all my time studying and more or less wanted to know about my progress every day. I reported all my pre-exam test results to her, and when she found something she could boast about to others, she did so, making sure Mansfield Cottage got an earful. I also noticed that a glass of milk and a cookie was left for me every morning, and this gesture took some getting used to. Glasses of milk and cookies were unheard of. I didn't even like milk, not having had it except in a milk pudding or my cup of tea, but I graciously thanked the housemother for her show of kindness, and most of the milk usually ended up in Ching's dish.

I didn't care much for the extra privileges, but the freedom was immeasurable, and I was able to bury myself in daydreaming and studying and eating whenever I wanted to. Someone once said that daydreaming was fine, if it came to mean something, so I dreamed on. My food was kept warm for me, and I was not expected to be on time for any of my meals.

It was at this time that I turned in a paper in my English class that caused some excitement. The headmaster of the school handed every girl and boy student in my class, their graded essay back but failed to give me mine. I did not know until much later that I had written an essay for a lead in to a story, which seemed to capture the attention of the headmaster who was teaching the class. I thought of myself as a future writer and storyteller, and for a while, most people had high hopes of a bright future for me. My housemother was in her element, and the buzz around the school took up momentum. Not having radios or newspapers, and with very little music except the hymns and carols we learned, I found out I could imagine and I could read, and I could be in a thousand places all at the same time with a myriad of things going on all at once. I couldn't talk in public and was too shy to hold a simple conversation, but I found I could write with feeling and put into words on paper what I couldn't otherwise relay to others.

I burned the midnight oil leading up to the final exams, talking with my teachers and wondering all the time whether I had grasped everything I had been taught and whether I would come through.

Our final efforts were tightly sealed and sent overseas to be perused by scholars unknown to us. If I did not succeed, there would be no point in continuing my education. I would either have to repeat the course in my nineteenth year or leave to try my prospects on my own, which was a daunting thought to say the least. I would not get my results until February of the following year, at which time I would have already been settled into the teaching college in Poona. I would have been mortified if, in the middle of February, I had to pack up and leave to go back because I had failed in my final exam. In my heart, I knew that, if I did not pass the exam, I would not go back but would look somewhere else to make a living.

The finals were over. I felt a little lighter and looked forward to the next chapter of my life. I knew where my mother was, secure now and close by, but I still longed for a connection with my father. Ivan and Rick were both in England with our father and his second wife. I am grateful that my oldest brother continued his support of us, through letters and cards, keeping up with our birthdays and giving us all the news of life in Great Britain. The subject of me joining the family in England never came up, but I was not ready to leave my mother and the rest of the family just yet. It was Mitchell's turn next, and he was in Calcutta, waiting for his departure date to England. This came the year after I graduated from Dr. Graham's Homes, when I was in my first year of teacher's training.

During the Christmas holidays, just before I went to St. Mary's Teachers'College, I was able to talk with my mother about my father. I tried to elicit some clarity—an explanation that would justify why he had been absent all these years—a very difficult task for her to accomplish. I began to see through the emotional fog that I was indeed growing up and that I needed to accept that my father's role in my life was over. I resigned myself to the fact that I would probably never see him again, although I eventually did many years later.

Questions rose up as I grew older, most unanswered at the time. What was this driving need that I had to keep my loved ones from harm? Why did I feel it necessary to lash out at people just at the mention of my father? Was there anything more overwhelming than the emotion I felt for my mother, even when someone had simply spoken of her? Unwelcome tears would flow down my face so easily, especially when I didn't cry at all otherwise.

Later I would come to a place in my life where I was able to sift through and wrestle with these difficult questions. When doing so, I would be able to go forward with my life to fulfill my dreams and find the peace I sought.

Chapter 17

During the last year at school, my fellow students became more likable, as we all matured and learned each other's limits of friendship. There was a mixture of Anglo Indians like me, Nepalese day scholars, one or two Tibetan boys, a Bhutanese student from a prominent family in the kingdom of Bhutan, and some Sherpa boys from the mountaineering families. We had become more familiar with each other as the years went by and learned how to laugh at each other's antics. We even went on field trips together that allowed us to talk with each other in a more relaxed setting. My female classmates and I particularly liked teasing the Bhutanese student who was quite shy. He took it all in stride and rewarded us with a grin whenever a present was left on his desk, mostly of the bug variety.

We had a lot of fun when we tried to teach the boys how to dance the Virginia reel and other square dances. A teacher from Scotland thought it would be nice to dress us in kilts and teach us to step lightly on our feet, as we skipped to the rousing Scottish Ballads. The senior graduating class gave a dance performance at the end-of-year awards ceremony. Most of the boys, being far removed from popular songs and dances of the outside world, did not have any rhythm. I have never had more fun than trying to get a six-foot-tall young man to hop from one foot to the other in time to music. No matter how much tutoring was spent on him, I never succeeded in teaching him the dance, so we had to perform without him. Most of us, including the Anglo Indian boys, took to the "highland fling" as though we were born to it, and we put on a very good show. I became good friends with some of my classmates and corresponded with a few of them for awhile after we graduated. But as happens with all friendships over the years, we lost touch when my travels led me far from the days of my youth.

A few weeks after we wrote our last paper, crossed the last "t," and put a full stop to the final answer on our last exam, my friend Sarah, myself, and a couple of the other classmates were relaxing in the senior class recreation room playing table tennis. There were only a few more days left before everyone would disburse for the end-of-year holidays and we would all part from each other to go our separate ways. The Saturday social for seniors was the last event for the year, and I felt nervous and apprehensive, knowing this would be the last time we would all be together.

I was fully absorbed in my game, so I did not stop to look at a group of people being ushered through the door by one of the teachers. My opponent stopped playing, turned to acknowledge the visitors, and stepped forward to greet them. I eventually realized there were others in the room and turned to see a group of young people being introduced as visitors from America on their way to Nepal. As I nodded to each one, my gaze slid back to a pair of deep blue eyes that seemed to draw me in for a closer look. Try as I might, I could not force myself to move on as I usually did when I met someone new. I turned to speak to Sarah, as she was being introduced as the captain, and found myself glancing at the stranger again. How could this be?

He stepped toward me, and I felt uncertainty take root deep inside me. I thought that, if he was looking for a likely prospect for conversation, it certainly would not be me. I felt the usual telltale signs of embarrassment and awkwardness coming to the surface and knew my face was turning red from my neck to the roots of my hair. I turned away to hide my shyness, and the next thing I heard was a voice asking me my name. Somehow, I heard the gentleman asking if he could be my escort to the Saturday social, and I said I would like that very much.

After a slight nod of my head, I silently questioned myself as I gave into the strange elation that came over me. Doubts surfaced at my ability to carry this through without falling apart. My escort was older than me by some years and quite attractive. Most of all, he spoke with confidence, and I listened to his lovely American accent, which fell pleasantly on my ears. I had to get permission of course, but a young junior housemother who had come to stay in Birissa Cottage gave her consent.

The first problem arose when I had nothing suitable to wear, and here the kindly housemother came to my rescue. When the day arrived, I borrowed everything and more, allowing myself the luxury of a shampoo and fashionable hairstyle, where my curls took on a shine all their own. I had roses in my hair and lipstick to match and felt very grown up in my borrowed pink dress and high-heeled shoes. My escort arrived promptly at six o'clock, and I was still walking on air as we entered Jarvie Hall for our last social.

All my schoolmates were there, and when I walked in with my escort, I saw nothing but approval and smiles from my classmates and other friends. All of a sudden, I felt that I was the most popular person in the room. I never lacked for dance partners that night, and of course I only had eyes for one person. The social evening was a boost to my confidence, and I was able to enjoy most of it. I loved to dance but felt more at ease dancing ballet solos and Indian classical rhythms and was rather stiff at first when my partner tried leading me in a two-step. A few whispered words of encouragement to help me relax, and I pushed the awkwardness away allowing myself to be guided around the room until I floated.

I was actually sad to see it all come to an end, and soon it was time for the slow walk back to the cottage. It was a lovely moonlit night, and we used the silvery light to find our way back, taking our time and holding hands. I didn't think beyond the moment, loving the new feelings that were going through me. In the back of my mind somewhere, I knew this would not last beyond a few days, but that thought was pushed out to make room for the wonder of it all.

We arrived back at my cottage, and as we approached the front veranda, the light streaming from inside the glass doors made patterns on the wooden floor and on us. I turned to my escort to thank him for the lovely evening, wondering if I would see him again. As he commented on the smallness of my hands, I wanted him to know just how much this evening had meant to me. Even though the words stuck in my throat and nothing came out, I found myself leaning forward to accept his gentle kiss.

Nothing that had come before or after felt quite like this. When I stood back from him afterward, there was a longing in me to step over the wall I had surrounded myself with and to find words that would allow me to express how much I liked being with him this evening. My throat remained closed, but for a brief moment, I felt an overwhelming pleasure and closeness with another human being outside of my family.

I was given permission to walk to the edge of the compound to say farewell to him. I knew that he would be gone the next day, as he would continue on his journey to Nepal. As we stood under the watchful eye of a beautiful full moon, away from the lights and shadows of the cottage behind us, I turned for a last kiss. I knew I would never see him again, but I was not quite ready to part from him just yet. I found my voice, and as I thanked him, he spoke touchingly of my youth, with years of life yet to live. His last words meant the most to me, when he said that, if he had brought me happiness in these brief moments, he would not ask for any more.

I had just experienced the most wonderful few days of my life with a stranger, and I was not going to let anything spoil this feeling inside me. I accepted his words, and because my expectations never went beyond just being with him, I was able to absorb everything. I treasured the goodness, happiness, and sadness and felt a total contentment for the brief and beautiful experience. I watched him go down the stony path, and his dark shadow disappeared around the pathway at the bottom. He had a long walk back up the hill to the Holiday Home about two miles away.

I turned to look at the Himalayan mountain range, outlined perfectly in the silver moonlight. I felt a gentle wind across my flushed cheeks, and I smiled, knowing my constant friend was watching and approved. I made a dash back toward the light streaming from the open windows of the cottage and, as I entered the front door, came face-to-face with the aunty. I was out of breath but full of happiness that I, the shy mouse, felt beautiful because someone had told me so. When it came time to thank my benefactress for her kindness just before I left Dr. Graham's Homes, she remarked on how she would always think of me on that night, with the light shining in my eyes, the bright color in my cheeks, and my head held high. I still dreamed of knights in shining armor, and this had been almost like one of my dreams come true.

I was eighteen years old and had yet to have my first drink, smoke my first cigarette, or have an intimate relationship. Until now, I was in no hurry to do any of these things. My Christian upbringing, sheltered childhood, and a good solid education throughout my life so far, were enough to see me through to the next chapter of my life, in which I would eventually experience all of these events and much more. I learned that I could makes mistakes, but I could also draw on the strong moral upbringing I had been given, and I was now in charge of my own life and destiny.

Chapter 18

I turned eighteen in the first week of December 1960. A few days later, I said good-bye to the only permanent home I had known since I was four years old. I looked forward to spending Christmas with my mother and siblings in her new home in Kurseong. After that, I would be gone for two more years, this time, thousands of miles away, across the plains of India. I would eventually graduate with a certificate of teaching under the European school code. This had been arranged for me by the most senior members of the staff at Dr. Graham's Homes, and I am forever thankful for their concern over my wellbeing and the kindness shown toward me.

Another student from Mansfield Cottage and I had chosen to attend St. Mary's Teacher's Training College in Poona. At the last moment, though, my classmate changed her mind and chose instead to stay home. Even though I would have liked to immigrate to England, as some of my school companions did, I had a strong sense of needing to stay in India. I wanted to do everything in my power to be there for my mother and help my brothers and sister carry on their education. I gave my support to them whenever it was needed. I knew by now how important it was for everyone, but especially for our family, to hold onto each other. I remembered the example my brother Ivan had left me—how he had been a solid anchor for my mother and younger siblings to hold onto. Being the oldest one left in India and the only one so far to complete all the education available to me at Dr. Graham's Homes, I took up the responsibility for them all. I saw Ashton, younger than me by a year and a half but smarter by far, complete his education to its fullest with accolades.

I spoke with Mr. Brooks, and furthering my education seemed to be the best decision I could make. I could think of no other way to make a living in India, since I was lacking in any skills. We spoke about the financing my tuition would take for the two years I would need to complete my course. I would stay at the college with a room of my own, along with several other girls. There was an account set up with the college bookkeeper where I would purchase books and much-needed supplies. He also informed me that I would not be expected to reimburse the school for any expenses incurred but elicited an agreement with me that I would return to Dr. Graham's Homes upon my graduation and join the teaching staff for two years. The pay would be minimal, as most of the staff of Dr. Graham's Homes dedicated years of their lives to the orphaned children and didn't expect many rewards for doing so. I assured the school principal and Mr. Brooks that I would return and help out in any way I could. I was deeply touched by the kindness that had been shown to my mother and myself and felt honored to be an ambassador for Dr. Graham's Homes as I continued with my education. I vowed to succeed in my endeavors and return a small fraction of the help I had received, even though I could never repay it all.

In the back of my mind, I wanted to leave my childhood and teen years behind. I believed that I needed to break free to explore the future and experience new places. I needed to give myself a chance to be on my own, to make my own rules, and to learn life's lessons. Still, part of me wanted to cling to what I knew, and I was hesitant about leaving the safety and security I knew to strike out on my own. I wished with all my heart that I was more prepared for life away from Dr. Graham's Homes. Everyone assured me that I was strong enough to push on, whether I knew it or not, and the Principal encouraged me to trust in my good common sense. He wanted me to remember that I had a good all around education on an equal par to any in the United Kingdom. He reminded me of the moral values that had been instilled in me throughout my life, of my knowledge of hard work and its rewards, and that I was capable of being an achiever. He stressed the need for me to be an example to my brothers, my sister, and many younger girls who looked up to me. Above all, he said I should trust in my Christian upbringing and love of God.

I was able to visit my mother a couple of times during those two years, traveling on trains and ferries. I enjoyed the two-day trip, during which I could look out of the window at the smoke-filled air rushing by. It was all I could do to avoid the coal dust blowing back into my red and gritty eyes, but catching the first glimpse of my beloved Himalayas was worth the noisy and crowded conditions. I could almost smell the cool, damp mists and fresh pine forests. I closed my eyes and waited for the familiar sensations to descend upon me like a security blanket. Sometimes, I would appear at my mother's doorstep after a long weary trip without a penny in my pocket. My shoes were scuffed and my feet blistered, having walked the last three miles from the town square carrying my suitcase. At the sight of her and my family, the song in my heart I'd first heard eight years earlier would be the only thing I heard at that moment. Her quiet greeting and little smile was all I needed. I would take a deep breath and inhale the aromas of the meal she was cooking for us. All the other dear little faces with their wide, open eyes would make my arrival as perfect as it could get, and I knew I was home.

Most of the time, I traveled throughout India on my own and was able to enjoy many associations with the people I met along the way. On some occasions when I had to travel, it was difficult to convince the authorities along the way that I was an Indian citizen and didn't need a passport to travel in my native country. I spoke the Queen's English, and everyone I met looked upon me as English, not Indian. Where a phone call to Dr. Graham's Homes used to suffice at the Teesta border crossing to give me clearance, it was now necessary to carry my baptismal certificate, as it was the only form of identification in those times. For the most part, I dressed in the European fashion, since I did not bear any resemblance to my Indian heritage and was looked upon with skepticism. That said, I had a good knowledge and understanding of Hindi, which helped me through many stressful situations.

I went on to complete two years at St. Mary's Teachers' Training College in South India, learning many of life's lessons along the way and making some lasting friendships. In particular, I met my lifelong girlfriend on the first day of college, and we became inseparable. An Anglo Indian like me, Lorna was from the suburbs of Poona and, therefore, a day scholar. She was extremely smart and had graduated from high school at the age of fifteen. On the first day, I saw a telltale twinkle in her eyes, a trademark of how she looked at life, and started a friendship that has lasted both of our lifetimes. With Lorna as my close friend, the two years of studying, with a good dose of fun in between, was life as good as it gets. I spent a wonderful day at her home, where I met her younger brother, Michael, and seven-year-old sister, Jennifer.

Lorna and I lost touch when I moved to America, but through today's technology, we reconnected several years ago through our daughters. I was extremely happy when I traveled to Australia in 2003 to see my friend after so many years. I had a glorious holiday with them all. Lorna now lives with her beautiful family in Australia, and we are still as close as sisters could ever be. Her children and mine have developed long-lasting friendships.

It was a period of much more freedom than I had ever known, of dating and meeting someone you later cared about so much that, whenever you saw him, the breath would be taken from your body. All you could feel was the pounding of your heart. I felt sorrow at losing that someone through separation and learned that life doesn't stop and wait for you to catch up. The slow-moving time of my childhood now seemed to be passing me by, and I was caught up in the swiftly moving events taking place all around me. The window I had been looking out all of my life was slowly closing behind me, and I had to step out from its shelter and look at what lay ahead. I peeked out very tentatively at first but soon learned to take small steps. Although I felt as if I nearly drowned sometimes, I always popped up to the top in time to catch the bright sun and fresh air.

I returned to Dr. Graham's Homes in 1963. I was twenty years old. I had to formally apply for the post of kindergarten teacher, and to my joy, I was accepted. I took up my teaching duties with energy and looked forward to being on the other side of life in the Homes. In the back of my mind, I thought about how lucky I was to be in an environment that was familiar to me, but I also knew that my destiny lay elsewhere, and I would have to go out and find it.

I was the resident teacher in Elliott Cottage, and joined the kindergarten staff. I settled in to two years of joyously teaching four- and five-year-old children of all nationalities. I volunteered and was nominated to be director of the Girls' Athletic and Swimming Programs, something that was very dear to my heart. We had two years of excellent games, and I learned how to organize and be a leader and mentor to others.

Chapter 19

At the end of 1964, I was twenty-two. I said good-bye to the beautiful mountain I had grown up on and bid farewell to all that I had ever known. Deep down, I was excited about the world outside but apprehensive about how I was going to tackle it. I had the means of securing a teaching position anywhere in India now, but staying close to my family was also important. After a brief Christmas holiday with my mother in Kurseong, I traveled to Calcutta, hoping to find some good prospects. Mitchell had immigrated to the United Kingdom by this time, and Ashton had just finished his last year and graduated with high marks, outdoing my not-so-great efforts. I stayed to help him find his own way, landing some interviews for him. Sometimes he was successful, and at other times, he was not. Not having any career skills posed a difficulty, and no outside help was available for a graduating Anglo Indian student. After our father sent for Mitchell, he didn't seem interested in the rest of his children, and this seemed to play on Ashton's mind more than anyone else's. He struggled with the sense of his father's rejection of him all his life and never came to terms with it. I always felt a loss myself as I watched my brother lose the drive and enthusiasm that was present all throughout his school years. I wondered to what heights of achievement he could have reached with the brilliant mind he was blessed with. Sadly, his father's rejection more often than not, led my brother down dark pathways with very sad consequences.

I took up a teaching position in Calcutta but found it increasingly difficult to find my own path to permanent stability. Finding a satisfactory flat to live in was next to impossible. I stayed at the Salvation Army for as long as they let me and then found a flat on the second floor of an old house, which was overrun with mice and cockroaches. The summer heat was intolerable, and I longed for the cool mountains and my mother and family. I tried to find the exciting Calcutta of my earlier years, but looking at it now with a newfound reality, I found desolation and squalor instead.

India was in the throes of political upheaval, especially on the northern border with Nepal, and the Chinese were taking over Tibet. The Kalimpong and Darjeeling areas were inundated with army posts and patrols. The area was becoming extremely restricted and open only to local residents. I was lucky to be able to get in and out of my own home. I looked foreign and ran into numerous unpleasant situations with the military patrols. Thanks to a major in the Indian Army who was stationed in Kalimpong and who was a friend to The Homes staff during my teaching years, I was able to eventually pass freely and without any more unpleasant incidents.

Before my departure from Kalimpong and with the help of the secretary of Dr. Graham's Homes, I was able to obtain a British passport and had been corresponding with my brothers in England to initiate the process of my immigration. It was 1965, and most of the year was over.

In the meantime, I was looking for work again when I ran into an acquaintance from Dr. Graham's Homes while browsing through the New Market in Calcutta. She introduced me to an American Marine from the embassy, who very soon advised me of a teaching position that was open for an English-speaking person. I jumped at the chance and found myself teaching conversational English to adult Indian women whose husbands were either attached to the American embassy or were professional doctors and lawyers by trade. I enjoyed my work tremendously and found the meetings with my students very rewarding, as we laughed and giggled our way through greetings and silly conversation.

When everything was ready for my trip overseas, events happened in whirlwind fashion. I found myself making the last trip back to the hills, to my mother in Dow Hill School, and there I felt all the uncertainty come back. I had never been faced with a more difficult and sad situation and the thought of leaving my mother and siblings ate away at my inner being. I was leaving my country of birth behind, not knowing for certain that I would ever be back. In the end, though, I said good-bye, made the trip back down to the plains, and boarded the airplane at Dum Dum Airport in Calcutta, for the first leg of my trip, which would take me to Bombay for the flight across the ocean.

Once I left Bombay and settled into the long flight to Paris, I gave a huge sigh of relief and let my tears flow. I was leaving the country of my birth and all that I held so dear. An overwhelming sadness settled on me. I loved this country I was saying good-bye to, but did I truly ever feel that I was Indian? I had lived in a sheltered world, raised by British housemothers and teachers. For the most part, I was schooled in the English language, with a class in Hindi and sometimes Bengali. According to my birth, I was Indian. In my speech, manners, and dress, I was connected to the English and did not have much contact with my Indian heritage for my first eighteen years. I had learned how to sing the national anthem in Hindi, recite the Lord's Prayer in Bengali, and dance to the beat of the *thablas* in intricate steps of classical Indian dance. I struggled with questions about my ancestry, especially upon leaving Dr. Graham's, and wondered where I stood in the grand scheme of things that concerned me. I was not yet comfortable in my own skin, and above all, I was traveling to a country where some did not recognize my mixed heritage.

As my destiny would have it, I did not tarry there long. I finished out 1965 in England and left in March 1966 to take up my new life in America.

In America, I was adopted with open arms and soon learned to accept the good in both my Indian and English worlds. I am very lucky to be a part of one of the most ancient cultures known to history and also one of the greatest empires known to man. My daughter, who is a first-generation American, is blessed with all the richness of these cultures surrounding her, and she has embraced them all.

Looking back on my struggle to find my own identity, I feel I was truly blessed all throughout my youth. I learned life's lessons, good and bad, from some truly memorable adults, some of who were dedicated to living out Daddy Graham's legacy of love and understanding guidance of the Anglo Indian youth. Could things have been done differently? Yes of course, especially in terms of not having the opportunity to experience India, our mother country. In a way, I felt that, by the time I was finally ready to embrace India fully she was not ready to embrace me, and being out on my own for that one year after I'd left Dr. Graham's Homes forever made me realize that the struggle would go on for quite some time.

Moving to America, and time, helped me to heal. I joined the best parts of my heritage and found peace in the two leaves of my existence, which came together. Beginning with my grandmother, the first bud has blossomed beyond my wildest dreams.

Author's Note

My childhood was spent in a community home located on a hill in Kalimpong, India, situated in the northern state of West Bengal. The home was founded by the Reverend Dr. John Anderson Graham, a Scottish missionary who, at a very young age and along with his bride, Kathryn, was posted out to the remote and rural hills of the Himalayas in 1886.

India was still under British rule at this time, and not long after settling into his missionary work, Dr. Graham began noticing children of a mixed race, unusual in these parts, living in the surrounding areas of the massive tea gardens and railroad construction sites. Traveling extensively around the area and making inquiries, he discovered that most of the children had British fathers and Indian mothers. He also observed that the children were being abandoned when their fathers were shipped back to their homelands. The Indian mothers, unsure of what to do, left their children in the villages as they traveled from one tea estate to the next looking for work.

Dr. Graham petitioned the Indian government and was granted a six hundred-acre site on Deolo Hill. Here he built Dr. Graham's Homes, a home for abandoned and fatherless children known as Anglo Indians. The first cottage went up in 1900, and forty other buildings followed over the next several years. A secluded, sheltered, mostly self-sufficient community emerged, with the glorious Himalayan mountain range as a constant backdrop. Mild weather and pristine surroundings made it an ideal location for the children, who grew up in a Christian environment, learning to work hard every day and achieving a well-balanced education that was set along the lines of any European school curriculum.

The children bestowed the name "Daddy Graham" on the home's founder, and this was what he was most proud of. To many of them he was the only "daddy" they knew.

For more information on the life and work of John Graham, I suggest reading *Graham of Kalimpong* by James R. Minto. The story of this great man is forever entwined with the children of the Anglo Indian race, who, because of him, were given dignity, identity, and the means of achieving an education beyond compare. Thank you, Daddy Graham.

"I Remember When ..."

Written by Yvonne Tomlin
Published in the *Scripps Treasure Coast Newspaper*
on January 1, 2012

I grew up in India, in the foothills of the Himalayas, in the late 1950s. I attended a little mission school with a tiny stone church and a small hospital on the hill.

One of my favorite memories was the Thanksgiving season. It was a celebration at the end of the harvest and of sharing this abundance with the local folk, who were poor and needy.

I couldn't wait for the last Sunday in November to come around every year. I would be so excited the week before, because all thirty children in our home would collect wild moss and flowers to decorate a wire basket, which would be filled with our Sunday eggs, to be given as an offering at the church service that day. As we all filed into the church on Sunday, I would always catch my breath at the sight of the beautiful vision of evergreen boughs, flowers, and colorful fruit and vegetables piled high on the altar. Loaves of home-baked bread were stacked in baskets on the side, all waiting to be blessed and thanks given.

At the beginning of the Sunday service, two chosen children from each cottage would walk up the aisle and place our basket of eggs in front of the surrounding harvest. There were always "oohs" and "ahs" as each basket was carried up carefully.

After the church service, all the high school children would join groups, and each would go off in a different direction. We would visit other poor children and their families living in makeshift lean-tos, hospitals, and dispensaries. We were also able to take food to folks living in the leper colony, on the outskirts of the village.

Tired, dusty, and blistered, I was never as happy as I was, all those years ago, to be able to bring happiness to so many who needed it. Their tears and gratitude are still fresh in my memory today.

My thoughts still return to The Kathryn Graham Memorial Chapel as they do every Thanksgiving Day, where I repeat this and other stories to my grandson, Thomas. His imagination takes hold at night before he gives in to sleep and sweet dreams, as he whispers to me, "What happened next, Yaya?" and I start with the words, "I remember when …"

Printed in the United States
By Bookmasters